WILL
YOUNG

TO BE A
GAY
MAN

1

Virgin Books an imprint of Ebury Publishing
20 Vauxhall Bridge Road
London SW1V 2SA

Virgin Books is part of the Penguin Random House group of
companies whose addresses can be found at
global.penguinrandomhouse.com

Penguin
Random House
UK

First published by Virgin Books in 2020
This paperback edition published in 2021

www.penguin.co.uk

A CIP catalogue record for this book is available from
the British Library

ISBN 9780753554258

Typeset in 10.05/21 pt Georgia Pro
by Integra Software Services Pvt. Ltd, Pondicherry

Printed and bound in Italy by Grafica Veneta S.p.A.

The authorised representative in the EEA is Penguin Random House
Ireland, Morrison Chambers, 32 Nassau Street, Dublin DO2 YH68.

Penguin Random House is committed to a
sustainable future for our business, our
readers and our planet. This book is made from
Forest Stewardship Council® certified paper.

To all the people who have pushed forward the LGBT rights agenda, I bow down to you and we all, as an LGBT community, stand on the shoulders of greatness.

CONTENTS

Introduction

I t's 7am on a crisp, autumnal morning. The sun is beginning to warm the honeysuckle, snaking around my window and filtering gently through my bedroom blinds, causing me to stir. There's the gentle hum of an electric milk float doing its rounds, purring away down the street. All is well in leafy south London, until . . .

'NELLY, PLEASE DON'T HUMP MY FACE!'

My two-year-old dachshund wakes me up every morning by placing her long sausage-like body across my face. Essentially, she attempts to suffocate me on a daily basis. This morning, such was her excitement, that her intentions became more amorous.

'OK, you got me; food time!'

That's it! She's off scampering down the stairs towards the kitchen. Esme, the Border terrier, follows in hot pursuit – carrying one of my slippers with her, I notice. This is my daily routine each morning.

Once recovered from potential 'death by sausage dog', I sit down, coffee in hand, to peruse the emails that have come in to 'Homo Sapiens', a podcast that I did with my best friend, Chris Sweeney. Scrolling down, I alight upon one from a 22-year-old in Finland who discusses his gay shame. It's a common occurrence, and seems to come up almost every episode. In fact, I'd just got back from America where we interviewed pop star, Sam Smith, who spoke of their own gay shame.

'That's it!' I proclaim to the dogs. 'I'm going to Google gay-shame therapy groups. There must be some in the world.'

The dogs don't care, FYI. But I do. Gay shame was a part of my life from the age of six. It has clung on to me like oil to a dying cormorant. It has literally stopped me truly flying in life. Years of hearing that to be gay was wrong, whether it be at a Bible lesson, in the playground, on TV or heard amongst adults, has wounded my very soul. The very essence of who I am has been defined as evil, disgusting and wrong. Growing up within a hetero-normative society has crushed my being. My gay shame, foisted onto me by others, has internalised and created its own gloopy tar-like substance, covering any light within. I have lived with a deeply repressed and under-explored belief that, by simply living, I am wrong and unlovable, purely by being alive. I've also realised I am not alone. So here I go! Let's see what can be done. Let's see what is out there. The answer is ... nothing.

Well, that's not strictly true. I come across an old work-shop, held in New York in 2016, which addressed gender norms, focusing on what it was to be a gay man or woman. This was, however, two years ago. My next discovery is far more interesting. 'GAY SHAME! HOW TO REDISCOVER YOUR TRUE SELF!' This is more like it. I enter the website and it's all looking good.

'Has your gay shame held you back in life?'

Yes.

'Do you want to rid yourself of this yoke and come back to your natural self?'

Another Yes.

'Then this is the programme for you! Get rid of your homosexual tendencies and learn to control your urges!'

HOLY SHIT! I realise I have unwittingly alighted upon a gay conversion website. Based in, well, the southern United States, of course. Now, such has been my own journey with gay shame that I am not triggered by this, but instead rather fascinated and amused. I decide to drop them an email.

Dear Sir or Madam,

Greetings from the UK. My name is William and I would love to start getting on top of my gay urges and homosexual tendencies. Please can you help me?

Yours shamefully,

William Young

All flowery writing and Googling aside, this morning is the morning when I decide to write a book on gay shame. As I've said, gay shame is something that I have lived through with every cell and fibre in my body. Even as I think on how I might approach this topic, ALL THESE STORIES start flooding back to me. ALL THESE MOMENTS of prejudice I experienced, and ALL THESE MOMENTS where other people's thoughts and feelings on what it was to be gay, and the shame that that's brought up in THEM, was dumped onto ME.

There were times, dear friends, when it almost destroyed me, but ultimately it did not, because I faced it and took it on. Through many years of facing my gay shame, I found strength. I reached out to others and expressed to friends and even strangers how I felt. Talking about my addictions, from porn to shopping, from failed relationships to always feeling less-than. I was spurred on by others' bravery in sharing their deep shame of themselves, and realised that I felt the same. Instead of feeling alone, I actually began to feel empowered. I cried a lot. I felt sick and ashamed a lot. And I heard a lot of other gay people's stories that helped me out of the darkness. But even through all of that, I was often the only gay person in a therapy group or indeed a treatment centre. It took time for me to find my own kind, where I could work through this specific issue of gay shame, and my development in abolishing gay shame was often sporadic and disjointed. Still, I got there in the end, and I'm here now to tell the story of just how I got there. I have no pretensions, but I come with authenticity, ownership, and a huge amount of hope and love.

Don't get me wrong. I am not so brazen or arrogant as to think that I know the right way to be gay; how could I? Everyone is different. What I want to do here is to track *my* life; to time-travel back to various times where knowing I was gay, or being gay, was difficult, painful, fun, terrifying, etc.

For me to be a gay man has been a constant journey from the age of four. It has involved so many layers of questions and internal wranglings, layers of shame that have turned into self-hate and loathing. To be a gay man has been a constant disappointment and occasion after occasion of embarrassment and hiding. In writing this book and using my life as a sort of blueprint, I hope that others might find moments of connection and resonance and perhaps glean some understanding and empathy for their own road through life. I know I have – it has led me to a newfound respect and admiration for myself and my sexuality.

Things that I'd completely forgotten about will, no doubt, surface, or perhaps things that have been triggering, but I'm looking forward to analysing and documenting how I survived them; how I got through school, and university, being at home, or even just hanging with friends. It's sure to be a weird process, but an incredible journey.

A journey that I'm inviting you to join me on ... and Esme and Nelly ...

... but to be honest they don't give a shit.

CHAPTER ONE

Bobby Not Pam

I magine being born into a world where, from the beginning, your true nature is under attack and ridiculed from the second you enter life. As you realise you are different to those around you, there is no place to find sanctuary. You become a prisoner to the constant barrage of shaming and disgust thrown your way. School is not a place of understanding; family holds the same negative views of who you are and the world itself holds no safety or place of refuge where you can be nurtured and supported. This is what it is like to be a young gay child in the world.

Of course, things have changed and I will not chastise every family by presuming they are narrow-minded. I certainly don't hold unprocessed anger against my family;

my parents did the best they could. They were progressive in so many ways and actually rather anarchic. I didn't hear constant berating of gay people and I have forgiven any ill words they might subconsciously and infrequently have used. It was what it was. With all this in mind, I take a deep breath and ready myself.

In the beginning I was born. My first awareness of being different was my sensitivity. I wasn't very sporty. I was very goofy and my knees knocked together when I ran. I was always transfixed by how beautiful my mother was, especially the smell of her perfumes and the sparkle of her jewellery. I would always notice the colour of whatever top or shirt she wore. She dressed well and I still remember her short hair, her African orange-stoned necklace, and the beautiful yellow sleeveless silk top she would wear with a long dark linen skirt. She was (and still is, I hasten to add) a petite lady; like Twiggy in the sixties. And to a little boy in the eighties, she was the most stylish and beautiful woman in the world!

I remember stealing one of her rings, which sat in a tin box with some other keepsakes. It wasn't especially valuable, but I became obsessed with it. It was silver and had a square black opaque stone set on the top. It was fairly chunky, actually, and its box sat on the windowsill in the bedroom I shared with my brother. One day, I opened it up and squirrelled the ring away under my mattress. I would get it out occasionally and gaze at it like Gollum in *Lord of the Rings*. Funny, it all seems to make so much more sense now.

Anyway, the long and the short of it was, I nicked the ring and said I had no idea where it was. Later that day, it turned up, back in its box, with me thinking I'd got away with it. It's only now, writing this, that I realise my mother, of course, knew exactly what had happened. It's like when my sister told me recently how heartbroken she was to learn that our father was only pretending to fall into the little booby traps we would set for him amongst the hay bales in our barn as children. My sister is 43.

I was not very coordinated as a child, I wore National Health glasses because of a lazy eye and I had a propensity to fall into water a lot of the time. I also spoke with a lisp; an attribute my father was not pleased with. It's strange because he isn't really a typical alpha male. He's tall and he has an incredible presence. He has a rich baritone voice and certainly has something rather mesmeric about him. He's very clever and very good at sussing someone out, as is my mother. He was never pushy for me to be a lad in terms of sports. He didn't play rugby or football in the garden with me. He didn't try to get me to do things that most other boys would do, but instead just let us kids get on with it.

I suppose because he travelled a lot, we didn't have as close a relationship as we could have, but when he was home my siblings and I would spend most of the time gardening with him. Daddy would tell me about what he was doing with the plants, and I would watch him for hours doing his thing in the veg patch. I would help with the mowing and dig up potatoes, sweep up leaves … hang on, was this simply child labour? Anyway, I really loved being outside with him and I learnt so much – things that have stuck with me, and remind me that I'm a country boy at heart.

I could be clever and say that what I was actually doing was trying to gain his love by being attentive to the thing he was passionate about. Perhaps he would feel pleased with me and forget about his displeasure at my lisp. I remember being in bed one morning; all of us sitting in my parents' room. My dad was determined to make me say my 's' clearly. 'Say it properly,' he would tell me.

I would try, but just couldn't. I remember getting very upset and my mother telling him to leave me alone. I mean, I could hardly call the social services over this incident. It is, however, an example of how a parent can shame a child.

My propensity to clumsiness, plus being very sensitive and prone to crying, didn't help my rather dim view of myself at that age either. In my mind, I was not a good boy. I wasn't living up to the stereotype of what it was to be a tough and robust young lad. It is common for gay men to feel like they can never gain the love of their father, and that they are somehow letting them down by not being manly enough. I don't have this. Aged five, however, I had no notion of sex or 'who' I was attracted to, but I was acutely aware that I wasn't what was seen as normal in terms of being a boy. I wasn't tough and I didn't engage in rough and tumble. When I cried my brother and sister would call me 'girl', and my God it was hurtful.

'Stop being such a girrrrrl!' they would say to me. I can clearly see the staircase in our family home, where I sat crying onto the bannister. The feeling was one of such sadness, and a desperate desire that I could and should change. I couldn't understand why I was so sensitive. I felt very ostracised. I remember feeling extremely isolated within the family system. I didn't relate to anyone else. I seemed to be the only one who was scared of strangers. I clung to my mother, and was easily set off.

Although this doesn't all necessarily relate to sexuality, it's a great example of a child not conforming to the usual gender norms, and how that can create a swathe of shame and self-disgust from a young age. Of course, there are lots of gay men who, when young and in adulthood, *do* conform to the stereotypes of being male: strong, aggressive, sporty. This can lead to a different kind of shame, where, as adults, they don't feel they fit into the gay community. As a boy who wasn't 'typical', I became 'atypical' and 'different' by default; I was on the outside. The overriding emotion that I remember wasn't self-hate, as much as it was confusion. I was terribly confused as to why I was the way I was.

It's common for young gay men to feel a sense of being different to stereotypical boys, through their lack of conformity. One of the most common areas, which can become extremely shaming, is sport, but sometimes the areas where a young gay boy might excel can also be shaming. *Well, of course you would be good at that because you're gay!* If you're young and sporty, then you're generally celebrated, but a boy drawn to more sensitive subjects – the arts, reading, theatre, dance etc – is often demonised. This can, of course, reflect society as a whole. Footballers and top sportsmen are lauded; they are our everyday heroes. Male pop stars who flaunt their heterosexuality are seen as the ultimate example of what it is to be male. Hollywood stars with rippling muscles, the guys who always get the girls, are seen as the pinnacle of success. The sensitive, weedy boy is always the fool; the one who gets picked on, the one who fails in life.

Aggression on the sports field is seen as fair play: 'GO ON, TAKE HIM DOWN!'; STOP ACTING LIKE A FAIRY'; 'WHAT ARE YOU? SOME SORT OF GIRL?'

These are the words that might be heard screamed from the touchlines by some parents, usually fathers, at their children. Even sports day can become traumatic for a child who doesn't have the desire, coordination or natural ability to run, or to hold a flipping egg and spoon! Surely if there were an atmosphere of understanding, nurture and celebration of all types of abilities, it would be a different event entirely. It isn't the taking part that's necessarily traumatic, although that alone can cause trauma; it's the atmosphere. In fact, an innocent school sports day can be an unsettling affair for a gay child. The overriding message for a boy who isn't winning in that arena is one of embarrassment and humiliation. This can permeate between parents as well. As one parent congratulates another, the parent with the winning boy might be subconsciously saying, 'It's a shame you've got one of those boys.' When the parents of the gay child are carrying their own prejudice about gender norms, this shame is swiftly passed on to their son, consciously or unconsciously. In fact, what a seemingly innocent sports day can highlight is that, as journalist and political commentator Owen Jones says, 'The people who suffer the most amount of homophobia are straight boys.'

If a boy is perceived as sensitive, the underlying worry is often that they might end up being gay. It is seen as the first sign of difference and therefore of weakness. One of the biggest insults that's used in the classroom is to be called gay.

Imagine if you are a young straight boy who, from an early age, is constantly called gay because he isn't sporty or manly enough, or perhaps even looks too pretty or is too thin. Two things can happen. Firstly, the boy takes on the shame of being gay without actually being gay. Secondly, the fact that he is being called gay even though he isn't can breed a deep homophobia within that child. The thinking being: 'If it wasn't for gays being so wrong and different, I wouldn't have to stand this abuse'. How can a child who isn't gay, but gets bullied for being so, ever grow up with a sense of pride and love towards gay people? It is seen as the ultimate defectiveness. The ultimate disability, and the ultimate crime. Of course, for young boys who are gay, it takes on a whole different level of shame and terror.

Even as I write, I have a sense of what that insult means. It is the end of the road. You can't go any lower than that. To be branded as gay is like saying, 'You're so wrong, you shouldn't even exist.'

This is how the chain reaction of thought goes:

If you are not fulfilling your gender norm, you aren't a usual boy. You are an embarrassment to me and my security in my sexuality and gender, because you are a living example of what it is to be a wrong boy. The social implications and signs are that you might end up not just wet and weedy but also gay. You are gay. You bring shame on your family. You are a pervert. You're disgusting, and you were made wrong.

I experienced this time and time and time again. One of my huge fears was to do with singing and my love of it. I was constantly worried that, because I had a high voice, and enjoyed singing soulfully, doing gospel-like riffs, people would see that I was gay. It's why I didn't sing properly until I was 22.

There is an interesting relationship between gender norms and gay shame. Anyone can suffer from gender stereotyping in childhood, as well as the humiliation that can ensue when you aren't the 'normal' son or brother or school kid. It is a short leap from that to homophobia. Indeed, we see it in the playground that so often the quieter, shyer boys are fast-tracked to being branded as gay; whether they are or not is immaterial.

There has definitely been a sea change in the last few years. Parents think more about what they dress their children in. We think more about how we gender-stereotype our children at school, in the home, and in general society. That's still not always the case, however. I went to a friend's house a while ago, where I put on their daughter's pink feather boa. She was seven at the time and their son was five.

'BOYS DON'T WEAR PINK!' both the boy and the girl crowed.

I so desperately wanted their parents to correct them. It's funny, because I believe underneath the fear of putting your children in anything other than what they are traditionally 'meant' to wear is the terror that they might be gay. I often ask myself, what is that terror? Where does it come from? A lot of it will be the worrying protectiveness over their children being different and therefore going into a world where they will be attacked, marginalised or at a disadvantage because they are not the norm. Sometimes, however, it's the parents dealing with their own prejudice towards having a gay child.

What will the neighbours think? What will people think of us? What will our family think? People at school? People in the street. Where did we go wrong?

The idea of visibility for a child who is in any way different to the norm sends some parents into a spiral. I get cross. They need to deal with *their* shit instead of putting it onto their kids. My cousin is friends with a family, who have a young boy who loves wearing dresses. I often see them when I'm visiting. His mother is an example of someone who totally has her shit together. She doesn't walk around with apologetic eyes or a fearful look. Her son wearing a dress is completely normalised, and she doesn't care about what that might turn out to mean. The other day, when we were both visiting my cousin, I showed him some pictures from the cover shoot for this book.

He said, 'You wear dresses but you aren't a girl.'

I said, 'No, I'm a boy, and I like to wear dresses.'

'Oh!' He paused. 'Could I see some more dresses, please!'

It's clear that this boy has free rein to wear, do and think and say what he likes. He's extremely well behaved and very comfortable. His mother shows us how a parent should be. As parents, we woefully let our children down by placing our own experiences of stereotyping onto our kids. By allowing young people to play with whatever they want to play with, wear whatever they want to wear, and be whoever they want to be, we let them live freely and express themselves. We sometimes get so confused and tied up in our own bigotry or terror of how our children will turn out, we forget to truly let our young people live.

*

Fundamentally, I feel that sexuality, and being gay, is still not being addressed in education, because, even now, people don't want to be seen to be pushing young people into a life of homosexuality. It's often still seen as a choice. On top of that, many parents simply aren't happy with the idea of their kids being taught about gay lifestyles or gay sex, as the 2019 picketing by parents of a school in Birmingham demonstrates.

According to the Alum Rock Community Forum, some parents temporarily removed their children from Parkfield Community School for *'undermining of parental rights and aggressively promoting homosexuality'*. A year before, I had interviewed the deputy head teacher of the school, Andrew Moffatt MBE, who, a gay man himself, explained that he had simply introduced a programme called No Outsiders. The ethos of the programme allowed kids to see diversity and difference, and helped them learn to respect it, even if they didn't necessarily agree with it. Within that, it promoted LGBTQ+ equality, and challenged homophobia.

I loved the idea of it, because the more children are shown difference in others, the more we all learn to embrace our own differences. You don't have to be gay to feel different; you might have additional needs or only have one parent. There are all sorts of reasons why a child might feel like they're not like everyone else in the classroom. You might be the only one who likes Brussels sprouts! It was the case, however, that the only thing that was covered in the media was the LGBTQ+ element of the programme.

The problem is that many parents just seem to concentrate on the sexual aspect of being gay. We're obsessed with sex, whereas six-year-old children are not. However, by ignoring the entire topic of LGBTQ+ people, we are lacking the initiatives to protect young gay people in schools. We are still not taking the issue of homophobic language seriously enough; it's often dismissed as 'boys being boys' or 'kids being kids', and that is not good enough.

It's quite simple. If a boy likes girls, and someone brings up the idea of kissing someone of the same sex, he might think it disgusting. The best thing to say to that boy is, 'Don't worry, you don't have to do it. You just have to respect the idea that someone else might want to.' I mean, I might find liver disgusting, but I wouldn't deny somebody else's right to eat it.

If a child uses the word 'gay' in a derogatory way, they might not think they're being homophobic, but the fact that it might be offensive to some people needs to be explained. Often, it isn't. The word gay, as an insult, and other homophobic language, is still rife within schools, and, unlike racist language, which is, quite rightly, stamped upon, it often goes unchecked. Parents sometimes argue that their children are being berated or punished when it comes to these issues, but in truth, they are simply being educated.

Where can a gay child feel truly safe? In the home, where they are different to the rest of their family? Out in the world, where they are at odds with the norm? In education, we need to make sure all kids are safe and recognised, especially the ones who are different. At the moment, the conversation around sex education and LGBTQ+ issues is at the discretion of the head teacher, but wouldn't a clear initiative be more useful?

Despite how far things have progressed, the issues around sexuality and being gay are still not taken seriously, so there are LGBTQ+ children who don't know what to do, and who are desperate for information and a way forward. Consequently, the percentage of young gay people with mental health issues is much higher than straight kids, with The Trevor Project (an American-based organisation providing crisis intervention and suicide prevention services to LGBTQ+ people under 25) stating on their website that LGBTQ+ youth are almost five times more likely to have attempted suicide compared to heterosexual youth.[*]

In 2018, UK-based LGBT rights charity, Stonewall, found that 52% of LGBT people said they had experienced depression in the last year, while one in eight LGBT people aged 18–24 (13%) said they had attempted to take their own life within the last year. Shockingly, almost half of trans people (46%) had also thought about taking their

---

[*] *CDC. (2016). Sexual Identity, Sex of Sexual Contaets, and Health-Risk Behaviors Among Students in Grades 9–12: Youth Risk Behavior Surveillance. Atlanta, GA: U.S. Department of Health and Human Services.*

own life within the past year of the study*. These figures are of epidemic standards and yet government response in the UK is woeful at best.

The process of my coming out was quite the journey, with failed attempts at sharing with people, and then going back into the closet again. It was actually a process that lasted 14 years. When I eventually got to that place of identifying as gay 'publicly', I was still not really out to myself. What I mean is, I wasn't comfortable with who I was, or my sexuality. I carried the yoke of shame for a good ten years more, at least. For me, coming out happened in three stages.

First, there was the realisation that I was gay. I did the maths, so to speak, noticed who I was attracted to as I grew up, and, as I became more sexual, I knew in myself that I was gay.

Second, there was the public declaration and sharing of my sexual preferences. It's weird writing this now as it seems so small. It's just one part of me; who I choose to

---

* *https://www.stonewall.org.uk/lgbt-britain-health*

love and who I am sexually attracted to. Yet this second part became a huge admission – and it really was an admission (although I don't like to use that word), such was the toxicity, guilt, self-hate and disgust boiling up inside me between stage one and two. It was tantamount to telling people I was a leper. A young boy who was defective in every way. For me, the nurturing that occurs in that period from stage one of coming out to stage two is crucial. If the person isn't shown that the world they occupy is safe – their family, friends, school, things they see around them in the greater world – and if these things don't resonate and vibrate with a frequency of love, acceptance and support, young gay people move into a fearful state, which can be a breeding ground for self-hate and loathing. The environment within which stage one and two happens is essential to how that coming-out process will go.

The third stage of coming out is what I call the 'integration stage'. It's where our inner and outer worlds merge and flourish. We need to feel the love of the world and experience our own inner love. It's an old simile but a good one.

After the egg, the butterfly has three stages: the caterpillar, the cocoon and the butterfly.

It is important to point out that these stages can happen very quickly. Someone could realise they are attracted to the same sex, come out publicly about it, and, dependent on their sense of support and self-love, might integrate all of it at once. I have to say I was not one of these people. My process from caterpillar to butterfly was more of a very slow undressing; taking off various items of clothing, while painstakingly making my 'carnival outfit' of wings with a Pritt Stick that didn't really work. Not only that, but I kept deciding to change the design as I went along.

I feel sad as I write, with tears running down my face. I can recall the feeling of desperation, hopelessness and fear, and I feel such empathy for myself back then. I feel empathy for all people who, through their sexuality and self-knowledge of that, have stirred up this infectious hateful potion inside that leads them to feel utterly alone and unaccepted by the world.

Thankfully, I now have my home, I have my job, I have my friends and, although I still find relationships hard due to past traumas as well as having a very dodgy nervous system that thinks it's about to be eaten by a tiger most of the time, I am at peace with my sexuality.

I realised I was gay aged around eight. It was all to do with Bobby Ewing in the American soap opera *Dallas*. He was the heartthrob, and I felt attracted to him while watching him on television. In my head, and also from what I saw all around me, I was clearly, as a young boy, meant to be attracted to his wife, Pam Ewing, but I realised that this wasn't the case.

It's interesting to me now how this had already started to become a hugely internalised thinking process. There was never ever the remotest idea that I would share with anyone, inside or outside my family, the information that I fancied Bobby, not Pam. The admission that I had a bit of a crush on the cowboy not the cowgirl. (I actually think my next album might be called *Bobby not Pam*.)

These days, it's hard to imagine being so withdrawn, and living this secret life with my sexuality at such a young age, but thinking back, I can really taste that climate of fear and confusion. The feelings of dismay at the growing amount of evidence that I was more than likely gay than not gay. Now, I want to be clear, I'd quite the burgeoning relationship with women. Between the ages of 5 and 7, I had kissed Sophie, a girl in my class, behind her parents' sofa. I then declared my love to Jessica Hanbury, who I told everyone I was going to marry. I was also going to have a Range Rover, be a vet and have Labradors. I was certainly performing to type in other areas of my middle-class life.

With Jessica, I think I would have been marrying above my station anyway. The Hanburys lived in a massive house outside our local town, Hungerford, and you could have fitted our whole house into their sitting room. Still, I take some solace now that they may have been richer than us, but their house was *right* next to the M4 motorway.

The wedding, thankfully, was not forthcoming. Once I started to fully get into the dramatic twists and turns of the *Dallas* plot, I knew that Jessica and I would never had worked. How far would we have got before I shared with her that I was more swayed towards double denim and a Stetson, over a pink off-the-shoulder full-length dress with frills on the sleeves? It would have been a disaster! So near yet so far from a Range Roger, five Labradors and a veterinary practice.

I'd trodden the 'normal' path of a young boy until Bobby Ewing. Now, as I look back on shows like *Dallas* and *Dynasty*, I realise it wasn't just the leading man I was interested in. The fights between Krystle and Alexis in *Dynasty* filled me with delight too, and the high camp of the show resonated with me.

It's funny, the question of what makes something camp and why it might naturally appeal to some gay boys. The answer still eludes me, but it illustrates how there is more to being gay than simply fancying the same sex. There are, if you will, certain traits and tastes that come to the fore. I'm generalising, of course, but I'm going to run through a few of them, things that I was already enjoying as a child.

I enjoyed pretty things, and what a woman was wearing: her perfume, her jewellery. When my mother was going out of an evening, normally a Friday night, she would come in and kiss me goodnight, and I would love the smell of her Chanel No. 5. She smelt so exotic. On one occasion, she had a short haircut – eighties Annie Lennox-style (it was the eighties so it makes sense!). She was wearing a mustard-coloured sleeveless top of fine silk, and a large African beaded necklace. She never wore make-up and looked beautiful. I was transfixed. From an early age I loved women's clothes and the way women looked. I would often buy my mother clothes for her birthday when I was a teenager: going up to London, looking in the shops, and buying things that I probably thought I would wear if I were her.

When I was at school, kids would have Pamela Anderson pictures on their wall, yet I cut out pages from *Vogue* and put them up in a handmade frame I'd rustled up in the art department. It was a clever ruse actually, because, like other boys, I still had women who I thought beautiful up on my wall yet I was more adoring of the clothes they were wearing, how their hair looked, and the general beauty of the art direction. I still remember now – Linda Evangelista in a Max Mara striped full-length dress, shot in the desert. As a teenager, I knew the names of all the supermodels from the nineties; not because I fancied them, but because I was transfixed by their beauty. I was amazed by how different they could look and also what they represented. These were women who became so powerful, famous and unstoppable. Cindy Crawford adorned many of the boys' walls in her Pirelli calendar shots, but I was more interested in Linda, Naomi, Kate, Yasmin Le Bon, Carla Bruni and Helena Christensen. They were siren-like, and swept the catwalks, descending like goddesses from on high. When George Michael shot the video for 'Freedom! '90', featuring all the supermodels, I could have died and gone to heaven!

Music is another trait that gay men can have in common and something else I loved. Especially the divas! Women who could properly sing, like Annie Lennox, who was an icon for me. She wasn't doing what other women artists were doing. She tested gender and the idea of how a woman could look. At the time, I never considered how ground-breaking she was; how she didn't represent the norm – but I think it must have seeped into me through her music. Her first solo album, *Diva*, wrapped me up and took me to a faraway place. I sank into the lyrics and the music of 'Why'. And it was Stephen Lipson, the man who produced that album, who was to produce my own first true album, years later.

Aretha Franklin was another diva I loved. Her duet with George Michael, 'I Knew You were Waiting', rocked my world. Joni Mitchell's more obscure albums *Chalk Mark in a Rain Storm* and *Dog Eat Dog* were on repeat on my Walkman, and I was a member of the Kylie fan club from day dot.

Books! I read a lot as a child, which is weird because I really don't now. I went through the obligatory *Famous Five*, *The Secret Garden*, *Charlotte's Web* etc. Then one day I stumbled across the Palomino Horse collection of books and no one could stop me. I raced through those books like a thoroughbred. It wasn't usual for a boy to read pony books, yet I did, and the fact I then moved on to Charlotte Bingham novels was even more interesting. Charlotte Bingham is predominantly known as a writer for a female audience. The weird thing is, I picked her book out myself, in a bookshop. My parents must have known, and, bless them, they never tried to edit my reading material.

My other fascination was also horse-themed: the TV show, *Black Beauty*. For those not old enough to remember, Beauty was a stunning black horse owned by a young girl who lived on a farm. Similarly to Shadow the sheepdog, Gentle Ben and Lassie, Black Beauty seemed to constantly sniff out troublemakers and, through some sort of magical symbiosis with his owner, managed to thwart any lurking danger. He was stolen, privy to bank robbers, thwarted loan sharks, and even managed to stop a gang of gypsies. (I'm not sure now if it was actually the most politically correct of kids' TV shows). I think there were even Russian spies involved in the plot at one stage, so the show was clearly doing its bit to fight the Cold War through children's programming, and subconsciously influencing a new generation towards a cultural bias aimed at the East. Black Beauty was also an Arabian stud, so quite how he managed to end up with an impoverished farming family was anyone's guess. All this aside, I loved *Black Beauty*. In fact, I always wanted to have that magical relationship with animals. I would go for walks and imagine my black Labradors were giant black horses, whispering to them about the secret goings-on of the Berkshire countryside. Hiding in bushes, I'd spy on the farmer as he went past on his combine, telling the dogs of his Russian heritage and intentions to take over our house. There was a time, however, when I moved from wanting a horse to actually becoming one.

My love for Black Beauty did facilitate an amusing (though not at the time!) story from my first year at my hideous prep school, Horris Hill. We would play on the bottom football pitches, which lay either side of the long drive heading up towards the main school. There were many days on which I would imagine myself walking up that drive and away from that hideous place, gazing longingly at it while waiting for my mother to appear in her black Ford Escort xr3i with red stripes down the side.

On this particular day it had been especially wet, and we were playing football. The pitches were at the bottom of a hill, so would get easily waterlogged. In fact, such was the poor drainage, it would often be like playing in a marsh.

It was a rare event that I managed to get the football, but that day I found myself at the halfway line with no one in my way but the poor, shivering boy in my opposition's goal. As I plodded along, tapping the ball towards the goal, the *Black Beauty* theme tune entered my head. I suddenly *became* the horse, trotting along, whinnying gently to myself, as the theme tune got louder and louder in my ears. As I arrived in the penalty box, I delivered my *coup de grâce* and swiped at the ball with my foot as people cheered me on. I completely missed the ball, but the momentum of my kick swept me off my feet and I landed squarely on my back in the muddy penalty box. The wind was knocked out of me, and I was left struggling for air and looking up at the grey sky, as the theme tune slowly died away. Black Beauty had failed me.

All these incidents from my childhood have helped formulate my opinion that being gay isn't *just* about fancying the same sex; it's often about having certain sensibilities. Fashion, women, smells, the arts, divas – you name it. Perhaps it's because these things are usually seen as girlish, and, being gay, that one's feminine side is more prominent. For me, this adds a richer inner layer to what it means to be a gay man.

CHAPTER TWO

Gay in the Eighties

Something that shadowed my entire childhood was the AIDS and HIV epidemic in the early eighties and how this was portrayed. It was seen as the 'Gay Plague', and used to such wicked effect against gay people: 'Look what they have brought amongst themselves. This is what happens when men sleep with men. Look what they have released on the world; an illness that could threaten humanity.'

The treatment and medical care for gay people with AIDS was sparse, hard to find and largely promoted by LGBT groups, charities and celebrity advocates for gay rights. Indeed, the building that now houses a well-known dance studio in Fulham was desired by Elizabeth Taylor to be used as an AIDS hospital in the 1980s. She was one of the earliest famous voices who stood up for the gay community and the illness that was ravaging them.

The combination of a world-famous pop star, Freddie Mercury, and this disease, was the perfect ammunition to highlight the miserable demise that awaited any gay man. The narrative was that gay men were salacious and sexually depraved, and this behaviour led to them catching this evil, almost biblical disease.

Interestingly enough, I always thought I would die of AIDS. My belief that I was evil had already been set in motion by Religious Studies. The story of Sodom and Gomorrah was the most damning of accounts in the Bible. It was a city that was rife with men having sex with other men. The story is used as a metaphor for the punishment against homosexuality. Indeed, the words sodomite and sodomise were picked up and used as pejorative terms against gay men, and inscribed into law, being used to describe sexual 'crimes against nature', specifically oral and anal sex amongst men – and bestiality! Yes, within the law, gay sex was put on the same level as bestiality.

The surrounding narrative was along the lines of, 'You're so evil that your type was killed by God in a blazing fire.' The rhetoric and descriptions that were used to describe gay men were not just descriptive terms, but pejorative ones that had their origins in something repulsive, cast off and depraved.

I remember watching, when I was eight years old, the television information films that were supposed to inform the public about the dangers of AIDS. These TV adverts were dark, involving approaching icebergs and volcanoes. The overriding concept was one of hopeless destinies towards an unstoppable natural disaster. The crashing and sinking after running into an iceberg, or burning alive due to a volcanic eruption. Each advert ended in the chiselling of AIDS onto a granite tombstone. The mood was anything other than light or hopeful. Instead, there was an atmosphere of doom and apocalyptic terror, and the overriding emotion that I came away with, after watching these adverts, was one of horror and fear. Of something that was 'other'; almost like an impending attack by alien beings.

The other thing I knew about AIDS was that it was created, caused and spread by gay people. It was an illness that gay men had, and it was their fault that the disease existed. I wasn't aware of anal sex at that stage, but as far as I knew, men could get it through kissing or getting naked with other men. If you were gay you had AIDS and if you had AIDS you could not be around other people. The illness was highly contagious and therefore you had to stay as far away as possible from people who had it. It reminded me of lepers, and from what I knew from the Bible, lepers had to stay in their own colonies. Their skin would fall off, they would ooze blood and pus, and you could catch leprosy by just being around them. Now, gay men were the lepers who had brought this terrible disease into the world.

Suddenly being gay – which I already knew was wrong and evil and made me a social leper – was laced with the risk of catching an incurable, catchable illness. Gay people were not just depraved and wrong; they now could kill you simply by being in your presence. AIDS bolstered the discrimination against the gay community and made it acceptable. It allowed people to shine a bright light on gay men's perverse actions and sexual deviance by showing a supposed direct correlation between their sexual acts and resulting demise. It was because of gay people that this disease existed and that it had been released into the wider community, and they were dying because of their choice to live their lives in such a hedonistic and repellent manner. Gay people released their 'Gay Plague' into the world, and the headlines blazed throughout the eighties: 'MY DOOMED SON'S GAY PLAGUE AGONY'; 'BRITAIN THREATENED BY GAY VIRUS PLAGUE'; 'I'D SHOOT MY SON IF HE HAD AIDS, SAYS VICAR'.

This narrative led to the even further segregation and disempowerment of gay people, bolstering and enhancing prejudice towards gay men across all avenues of society.

People who contracted HIV and AIDS were seen as victims; helpless and doomed. They were all made out to be lost causes, suffering intolerable pain and misery and despair. And because the majority of people who were most likely to catch the illness were gay men, drug users, or women in the sex profession, the notion was that it was their own fault in the first place for being depraved. They were not worth allocating funds to, and the world was a better place without them.

Healthcare in the US and then UK was slow to help anyone with the illness, and governments were unwilling and resisted spending money on finding a cure because the social group who contracted it were generally seen as morally bankrupt. In fact, for a while in the early eighties, HIV and AIDS was mislabelled as the 'Gay Related Immune Deficiency' disease. The stories of how people were treated during that period are too many to count.

Speaking in the *Independent* in January 2017, Michael Penn from the Terrence Higgins Trust remembered how after his partner died, he went to his local pub, and the barman, knowing his boyfriend had died of AIDS, ordered that no one else should touch the glass that Michael was drinking out of. This kind of misinformation allowed people to look even more suspiciously on gay men. The lack of information and education led to a rise in fear of gay men, and fear always leads to prejudice if unchecked.

Growing up, HIV and AIDS made me think I was destined to die young from an incurable disease, and it would be my own fault. I imagined I would automatically catch it from sleeping with another man. The lack of education in schools focusing on STDs and prevention of AIDS and HIV meant that I bought into the story I was force-fed in the eighties and even the early nineties. I felt filthy, but also trapped. Subconsciously, I was condemning myself to die by fancying and loving people of the same sex. I was performing the ultimate treason; turning against life by choosing to love men. Not only was I evil and destined to go to hell, but I was also going to deliberately end my life due to my choice, desires and faulty genetic make-up. AIDS and HIV brought up a whole other level of conscious and subconscious beliefs in me. It was yet more evidence that who I was in my essence was wrong and it reinforced my belief that I was damned in this world and the next. In fact, the sense of hopelessness and helplessness is not just indicative of the shame I felt, but is also the very definition of trauma. Trauma is to feel oneself in a situation that is entirely hopeless and one is powerless to do anything about it, and as far as I was concerned, I was on a crash course towards utter rack and ruin. The worst thing was, I couldn't do anything to stop it because it was *me*. I was the problem. I would die alone, with no children, cast out by my family and friends and society, and I had no one to blame but myself.

Recently, I invited Peter Tatchell for tea to discuss all this. Peter lived through the AIDS epidemic, and knew the narrative first-hand, and how gay men were treated, which was dictated by a heteronormative and bigoted government.

'To begin with, there was little to no information,' Peter told me. 'When gay men were dying, the mainstream media weren't interested. It was thought HIV was possibly caused by poppers. It only hit the big time in mainstream press when the first heterosexual person died of HIV. The dialogue that was then created by the media was that it was a gay plague that threatened us all.'

Peter went on to talk about what it was like to live through this.

'Imagine living through it – our lives are worthless; they are going to let us die, was what we thought. They wanted us dead. Some people had the view that the disease was deliberately allowed to flourish to kill us off. The government at the time under Thatcher was homophobic – "the family values" and "Victorian values" campaign, with the directive by Thatcher that we had to return to traditional family morality and life, and sexual freedom was wrong and had to stop. One Conservative councillor said that to stop AIDS all gay people had to be rounded up and gassed. Two friends of mine were regulars to a local pub and the landlord said from now on you have to bring your own glasses and cutlery.

'There was a famous case of a gay guy, who'd been taken to court for some reason, and the judge ordered for him to be dressed head to toe in a boiler suit and mask and everything burned at the highest possible temperature afterwards.'

Peter's book, *AIDS: A Guide to Survival*, is a fascinating and imperative look at what went on during this time.

He investigated so many events and policies percolating beneath the surface of national-and local-level governance.

'The chief constable of Manchester said that "gay men were swirling round in a cesspit of their own making." The practice of the police raiding gay bars with rubber gloves arresting people for gay sex was possibly a consequence of this writing and thinking.

Rising homophobia supported by a Conservative government, followed by the introduction of Section 28, which prohibited local authorities and schools from 'promoting' homosexuality, saw a huge spike in gay attacks and murders.

In his book *AIDS: Don't Die of Prejudice*, Norman Fowler, the then government health minister, concedes the government response was late and it was seen as a moral issue not a health issue. Indeed, it's astonishing to hear Peter talk about how openly attacking and prejudiced the eighties and nineties were under the Thatcher government. There was little to no help or pastoral guidance during the AIDS crisis, and this undoubtedly led to a bolstering of homophobic beliefs, which were rolled out onto young gay boys like myself. The rhetoric and dogma were that it was debased, wrong and even caused deadly disgusting illnesses. Speaking to Peter allowed me to see how cast out and alone the gay community was back then, yet at the same time, the community came together to help themselves. It is through this kind of connection and loving support that we can work through our gay shame and thrive, rather than simply survive.

There was also a severe lack of gay role models during the eighties and nineties, which is why I believe that the visibility of people who represent us is of vital importance. When the film 2020 BAFTAS were announced, the head of BAFTA was gracious in her acknowledgement that the list of nominees wasn't as diverse or representative as it could be and had been in the previous couple of years. It is perhaps also interesting to point out that in the category for best actor, the person playing Elton John in the biopic *Rocket Man* was straight and later went on to win a Golden Globe for Best Actor in this role. Last year, the actor playing Freddie Mercury in the biopic *Bohemian Rhapsody* was also straight and won the Oscar for best actor.

As an actor myself, I find myself falling into an internal conflict over this. What I find interesting is that often, when a straight male actor plays a gay role, they receive such plaudits, praise and often awards. It is seen by the heteronormative world as such a remarkable transformation and such a 'brave' thing to do – to be sexual with another man – as if they should otherwise find it repulsive and shocking. Incidentally, I had to kiss a woman in a TV series I was in. It wasn't hard, it wasn't terrifying and I enjoyed it; it was bloody funny. No one asked me about what it was like to be so brave and challenged by kissing someone of the opposite sex. Now I am not Hollywood-level; however, so often we see heterosexual men being bowed down to for stepping into the role of playing a gay man. *Brokeback Mountain* had two straight men playing the roles of cowboy lovers, and both were nominated for Oscars. I am not chastising the actors, but consider the lack of gay actors who are cast into straight roles, and then oddly not cast in gay roles either. Do people think that gay actors aren't acting if they play gay? That they are simply being themselves?

On a day off recently, I was sitting in a hotel, visiting my friend, Mark. The hotel was comfortable and decorated well. Around the bar on the walls was a painted mural of a party scene: sort of cocktail-evening-inspired; with a 1940s feel. What I really noticed is that there were no black people in the scene at all. I guess I was thinking of Afro-Caribbean people specifically because two members of my band are of that ethnicity, and there was also a mixed-race couple near me at the hotel at the time: the woman was white and the man was black.

As I sat there, I wondered what it must be like for a black person, walking into this hotel and seeing no representation of themselves on the walls. What feelings would arise? A sense of not feeling welcome, I imagine. The idea that this place isn't for you. Feeling like an intruder into a life or environment that is inhospitable. Feeling like an outsider. There is no sense of comfort or safety. I feel different and an oddity. Looking at the walls from this perspective allowed me to access this feeling and relate it to being gay.

Of course, the history of abuse and disempowerment and illegitimacy of being black throughout the
world is entirely different to being gay, and I would not
for a second propose that it is the same because it would
completely negate any feelings of what it is to be black.
One of the primary differentiations in day-to-day life is
that one cannot hide the colour of one's skin, whereas, as a
gay man, one can live in the shadows and live a lie behind
a mask. What I accessed is that feeling of being an oddity
as a gay man. By not seeing any representation or visibility even in such a simple example as a mural on a wall, I
feel 'not the norm'. The norm of having fun, drinking and
socialising within this space does not include the likes of
me. This hotel is not for me and my gay friends to partake
in, or if we are to visit and have fun, we must hide who we
are. It is effectively not a safe space.

If I translate the example of my hotel to the wider
world, it is no different. Where did I see gay people when
growing up? Where were gay storylines in films? Where
were the gay posters and actors? Where were gay people
in my social circles when growing up? What was the narra-

tive and discourse about gay people and their lives? There was next to nothing.

It is essential that we see who we are represented in all areas of life. Be it female directors, black actors, or more diverse and inclusive stories. This is how we all learn, and can be inspired. We see that we can be more than the stereotypes thrust on us by a patriarchal society that seeks to limit and control. Growing up, I lacked these stories. Gay men either died of AIDS, like Freddie Mercury, or were portrayed as sordid and lewd, 'discovered' in public toilets, like George Michael.

There was another type of gay man on TV when I was young, who I like to call the clowns. Often, they were gay men who were allowed to appear on TV to camp it up, but restricted to playing the formulated 'Carry On' role: Larry Grayson, Frankie Howerd, Kenneth Williams. These men were there for the puns and double entendres. A sparkly jacket would suffice, and oddly, they became sexually neutralised.

Gay men in the 1940s were allowed sanctuary in the theatrical world. It was seen as one of the safe spaces as long as it was never openly addressed. In television and light entertainment, gay men were safe as long as they were playing the jester; entertaining us yet never challenging us. The role models for me growing up, therefore, were basically repressed gay men who danced to the tune of the heteronormative bureaucracy for the entertainment of the audience at home. That wasn't a life I wanted.

These days, TV regulars like Graham Norton occupy a fantastic position, seen as being funny as well as intelligent and authoritative. However, there are still many light entertainment shows that portray homosexuality as something a bit risqué. Something that perhaps warrants a little laugh, but is kept firmly in its place.

Aside from light entertainment, people who supported gay causes and appeared on more serious programmes, discussing social topics, were often ridiculed. Peter Tatchell, who is an activist for human rights across the board, and who has fought for gay rights for over 50 years now, was absolutely vilified. The narrative I got when he was on television was that he was an irritant; someone who banged on about insignificant topics such as gay rights.

At the time, I felt internal disgust and couldn't identify with him. Peter didn't live in the protective bubble of pop music, where one could accrue a mobile and supportive fan base who would give you credit. He had none of that. He existed on the front line, which is why I now look back on what he did with huge admiration and wonder. He publicly spoke out on platforms, sharing TV shows with people who would quite openly call gay men 'poofters', 'faggots' or 'queers'. I salute him!

In terms of role models, I firmly believe that had there been people such as Olly Alexander, the frontman of the band Years & Years, or an artist like Christine and the Queens – both embracing and living authentically in their true selves – I would have shed some of my shame. I'd have seen that there were people out there who were not just freaks and there to be sneered at, but were success-ful and proud. Their light would have shone out to me, and perhaps inflated my own self-belief and confidence in being alive and existing in the world.

CHAPTER THREE

An Education

After leaving Horris Hill Prep School, aged 13, I went to Wellington College. It was daunting to go from the top of the pile in one school, right back down to the bottom, as was leaving all my friends behind. I was fortunate in that, being twins, my brother Rupert and I were in the same year, and in the same boarding house. It was the same one – The Hopetoun – that my father had been in, back in the sixties.

With schools like Wellington, if you had a parent who'd gone to the school, it was felt you were more likely to get a place. As well as this, my father had been rugby captain, which held a certain cachet as Wellington was big on rugby. I clearly remember my first day there. The night before, I'd gone into my parents' room, crying and saying I didn't want to go. They told me to give it until half-term and see how I felt then. This placated me somewhat, although, looking back, I just didn't want to go to boarding school. After Horris Hill, however, Wellington was like a holiday camp. We could wear our own clothes out of the classroom – so from 6pm in the evening and at weekends. There was a full-on sweet shop called Grubbies. We could listen to our music (music at Horris Hill was limited to three hours a week) and we were called by our first names.

Still, I found the first day terrifying; the older boys looked like full-grown men! And with thoughts of my sexuality always in the background, I was curious and nervous as to whether being gay would 'stay with me'. Meanwhile, I, of course, developed crushes on some of the other boys. New students turned up a week before the rest of the school, except the top two senior rugby teams, who would train for the whole week. I remember on the first day, having an 'orientation' morning around the school. As we got down towards the rugby fields, I had never seen anything like it. I felt like I was watching the giants amongst boys, who actually resembled young men. Naturally my eyes went to the 'young men' who I found attractive. One of them, incidentally, went on to become a Calvin Klein model, so I suppose I had some sort of good taste. I felt utterly daunted and thrilled, yet also wrong, almost depraved, that I was attracted towards people of the same sex. It was like I inhabited a whole other world – an inner world – of desire, fantasy, love and attraction. It was a world that I could and absolutely would not allow ANYONE else to know. At times, I existed there completely, yet no one knew. It was comforting in a way, but thinking back, I was living purely in my head, and the utter commandment was that I always would be.

It was around this time that the internet launched (which makes me feel extremely ancient), and I realised that I could now get online and watch gay porn when I was at home. This was a revelation, but not always easy to achieve. Firstly, I would have to sneak out of my room at night and go to the spare room, where the computer and router were kept. Once there, I'd have to put a towel over the router because it would make a noise like a fax machine as it 'dialled up', which lasted for about 30 seconds. I cannot explain to you how excruciating those 30 seconds were; the noise that bloody router made was like a ghostly cat screaming through a fan. I would sit with bated breath, waiting for the horrific sound to finish, and then, as quickly as possible, search 'gay porn'. Then in darkness, lit only by the glowing computer screen, I'd wank as quickly as possible. It was what you might call a danger wank!

There was, I suppose, a sadder side to it, in that I felt so terrified in case I got caught, as any teenager would. The truth was, I couldn't find gay porn anywhere else, and didn't yet have the confidence to walk into a newsagent or sex shop to find it.

Prior to my discovery of porn, stimulation had been scant, although there was the Chippendales video that my sister had been given for Christmas. The Chippendales were an American act made up of male strippers, who, during the eighties, became huge, selling out arenas. They were all oiled, with long, wet-look perms and G-strings. It's not something I would find sexy now, but at the time it was very arousing. Again, it was all I could get my hands on, aside from a video copy of *A Room with a View*, starring Helena Bonham Carter. In the film, there was a famous homoerotic scene where three of the men went skinny dipping in the woods, and then ran around the edge of the lake with their knobs out. The sight of a young Rupert Graves – who, years later, I recorded a radio play with about a woman giving fake birth to baby rabbits – was too much for me, and I would slowly frame-by-frame move this scene on using the pause button. Afterwards, I would have to make sure I rewound the video back to the exact time-mark it was at to begin with. I chose not to share this information with Rupert Graves, which, I think, was probably for the best.

At that age, even uttering the word 'gay' was something I found excruciating. It was literally impossible for me to even formulate the word and and say it out loud. The use of the word 'gay' was like uttering 'Voldemort'; it was so wrong, and so dangerous, that the implications of saying it were utterly catastrophic. Even after coming out at university, I'd been so conditioned to the foulness of the word that it took me another ten years to get comfortable with it.

My first experience of telling someone I was gay was when was 16. I was at Wellington, and it had all been building and building inside me, to the point I was beginning to get depressed for the first time. I wasn't in utter devastation, but it was noticeable that I was not my normal bubbly self. I remember sneaking up to my friend Andrew's room, which was two rooms up from my and Rupert's room, on the same corridor. Weirdly, I remember I was wearing a green Emporio Armani shirt, which eventually joined the long list of lost clothes I will occasionally mourn for. Once there, I told Andrew I had to tell him something, but it took me so long to get it out. I remember crying a lot, and getting super super hot and sweaty. I finally managed to get the words out, but thinking back, I don't know if I actually said the word gay, or rather alluded to it. Andrew was invaluable to me at that time.; the first person I felt wasn't judging me. I will forever be indebted to him.

After that, we set about testing my sexuality, by seeing how I fared with various friends of his girlfriend, which now actually sounds a little bit creepy. It was a bit like a science experiment, I suppose. I remember the first party I went to, which was at Andrew's girlfriend's house. We turned up to find about seven girls, and we all sat around the sitting room eating pizza. I am not shitting you when I tell you that we watched the 'Greatest Love Scenes from *Neighbours*'. It was one of the worst and dullest evenings I have ever spent. I ended up sitting in the dog-bed downstairs in the kitchen, with the family's Dalmatian, who was adorable and, like me, had little interest in watching Kylie and Jason break up again.

Andrew actually did wonders for alleviating some of the pain and terror I had bottled up inside; it was a tougher job, however, to dig out the deep shame that had settled in my system.

By the time I was 16, everyone at school was getting a bit more sexual, and it was fascinating watching some of the boys I knew move slowly into their sexuality. Wellington only had girls in the top two years, and it was often the most unexpected of boys who would suddenly be dating one of them. There was a confidence that came with my peers as they paired off with various girl students, but it wasn't just within the school that they'd meet. We had what we called socials, where one year of students would go off to a girls' school and have a dance with them. Alcohol was, of course, always smuggled in, and someone would always get in trouble. I'd never go, but back at school, I'd be eager to hear all the stories of who had got with who, and how far they got. One of the Wellington boys ended up using loads of French bangers to blow up one of the girls' lockers. After that, and possibly to this day, Wellington was banned from attending the socials.

During this period, I created a sort of character for myself, and, in a way, became untouchable. I felt like I had everyone under my control within my boarding house. I was suitably subservient to the boys above me, I respected the boys below me, so they respected me, and my housemaster adored me. Outside the boarding house, however, I was effectively mute. It was a strategy that worked. I wouldn't talk to anyone and so gave them nothing on me. I still use this strategy sometimes. It's better to keep one's head beneath the parapet and let one's actions do the talking. That is how I have approached my singing career, right from the beginning.

It was sport that initially gave me some kudos, enabling me to branch out from the boarding house. From the age of 13 onwards, I practised at the basketball courts constantly, and watched all the older boys playing. I learnt a lot, and slowly got better and better until, aged 16, I was in the starting five for my year. Suddenly, through basketball, I was allowed into the 'cool gang' (with a group who called themselves 'the Asian Posse!'), where my sporting prowess gave me huge points for being 'manly'. It was a brilliant coat of armour, but I also found joy in it. When I talk of my sporting capabilities, it's not with an intention to brag; post-puberty I started to see that I was actually a good runner, my physique started to develop quite quickly and I became stronger and in turn more self-confident in my abilities in sport. It is, however, an example of how people's narrow way of thinking about what a gay man could be allowed me to thrive, while also throwing potential bullies off the scent, so to speak. It was the narrow stereotyping from a heteronormative society that gave me the camouflage I needed. How could someone who plays a sport so well and so physically be gay? He couldn't!

In the Asian Posse there was Emil, who was extremely wealthy, Deshan, Tayo, who was an incredible athlete, my brother Rupert, and me. At Wellington, basketball was a bit of an unknown. It existed in its own bubble, where I managed to create a protective oasis around myself. Firstly, due to the American cool factor that the sport brought, we were allowed to walk around in baggy shorts and vests. Secondly, the kind of game we played was rhythmic, flowed and, basically, few people could play it. The 'lads' in the school lacked the dance-like coordination required to play it well, which is why we were respected and, in a way, feared, because once on the court in inter-house matches, we had the ability to shine and make others look less-than.

The other protection I had was racial. People couldn't really challenge the identity of my friends in the Asian Posse. Yes, they were in the minority, but it was very different to someone identifying as gay. This was race, and people were, without doubt, wary of and intimidated by them. Emil was the son of a sickeningly rich family. Nazif, another friend, was known for being very strong. Tayo was also from a hugely wealthy family, and Deshan challenged everyone's limited views by being incredibly gifted in all three top sports – hockey, rugby and cricket – while also being very hippy-like in his approach to life. All four boys didn't take any shit. Boys older and younger were wise enough to know that it would be foolish to go up against them. On the rare occasions when somebody did, they were quickly, and physically, shut down. I had unknowingly created an enormous protective buffer against anyone who might get as much as a sniff of my gayness. It was another opportunity to throw people off the scent and hide my shameful secret.

It wasn't all plain sailing, though. On one occasion one of my own school friends shot me down in front of everyone, uttering the unspeakable.

This friend was was an incredible athlete: tall, lithe and rippled with muscles. He was also, I came to learn, a cruel and unpleasant character who preyed on people's weaknesses. On that day I came into the dining room at school, aged 16, wearing my basketball vest. I was fortunate to have a naturally athletic figure, and knew my arms looked good in a vest. It might not have made me cool, but at least I could boost my self-esteem by looking in the mirror.

Anyway, I was just sitting down when he looked at me across the table and said,

'You know, I think your parents must have been on steroids when you and your brother were born. You both have brilliant bodies and look ripped.'

So far so good, but somehow I knew it wouldn't last.

'The thing is, Will, you look all manly, like you could beat someone up, but then you open your mouth and this soft lisp voice comes out,' he said. 'It's almost as if you're gay.'

As soon as the words passed his lips, it was as if I'd been kicked in the stomach and had fallen to the ground. The feeling I had was utterly depleting; full of overwhelming shame. The notion that someone had seen through my disguise was terrifying, and from then on I walked on eggshells with the terror that someone might see the real me. The me who was absolutely repulsive to his core.

With this hanging over my head, I decided to tread a tightrope along which I would deftly walk, attempting to balance an outer projection of normality yet never completely throwing away my authenticity as a young gay man. It was exhausting living a lie, absolutely exhausting, and I can sometimes still experience this feeling when I am having an episode of anxiety or depression. It is a balancing act between containment i.e. not splurging out my emotional state at any opportunity, and also being true to myself at any one time. Mental and physical health, however, are very different to living in an environment that is fundamentally not safe and not accepting of my very essence and being. When I was a teenager, it was like living behind enemy lines. The truth being that it felt as though even my friends were the enemy.

Wellington College was a beautiful old building made up of lots of courtyard and quads, each with a different name. I lived on the edge of the school's grounds, so after tea on a Friday evening, I would cross the lower

Combermere Quad into the Back Quad to where the rugby fixture lists were posted, to see whether I was playing away or at home that weekend. I had another agenda, however, which was to see which of the other boys were playing on the away teams. Perhaps I would get a chance to see some of the boys who I fancied, naked in the showers. The trouble was, thinking like this would lead me to feelings of self-disgust, reminding me that I was living a lie and masquerading amongst my peers. I chastised myself, attacking myself as some sort of pervert. I took on the thoughts that all the straight boys would think of me: 'Oh, when Will tackles boys on the rugby field, he's obviously deriving some sort of sexual pleasure from it.' I attacked myself endlessly. It must be horrific, I thought, that these poor boys had someone like me in their midst. I felt almost as if I was predatory. The thing that crippled me even more was taking showers with other boys while on away rugby matches. What would happen if they eventually found out I was gay? Surely they would be looking back on all the occasions I'd seen them naked, with anger and repulsion. The idea that I could move undetected in their midst, showering naked with them, and, even worse, getting sexually turned on by the ones I fancied. I was racked with conflict. On one hand I was following an urge that was completely natural to a teenage boy. Imagine if I was heterosexual and had the opportunity to go away with a whole selection of girls my age *and* got to shower with them. No one would see my excitement and sexual desires as anything other than natural. In fact, I'd probably be applauded for my expression of sexual prowess and development into becoming a man.

However, what if people knew that I harboured sexual desires and crushes on a certain boy? Or that I would masturbate back in my room with stored-up visions in my head of boys I had seen naked that day, soaping up their bodies. Boys whose willies and bums I had seen, before turning the images into my own secret fantasies. If people knew all that, it would surely be completely acceptable for them to cast me out, to beat me up, to insult and torment me. After all, it hadn't been that long since being gay was still illegal.

I feel it's important to stress that I don't think of any of these things now as a 41-year-old man. What I mean is, I am not writing these memories, lasciviously thinking about 17-year-old boys. I am writing about how I felt then, and how my natural sexual desires played out. It's in itself interesting that I feel the need to say this. On the one hand, it is entirely appropriate, but on the other it is perhaps a reaction to how gay men have been vilified in the past, and how being gay was often linked with paedophilia. Being gay often meant that one was seen as predatory to all males, no matter what their age. In fact, I believe the notion was that a gay man couldn't overpower a straight adult male, but could easily prey on the vulnerable and physically weaker, who were young boys.

The other factor that didn't help these blinkered and damaging views was that schools and the education system could be a breeding ground for gay men who *were* paedophiles. I certainly experienced some predatory men when I was younger, but it wasn't always clear if they were men whose massively suppressed sexuality had compelled them to prey on young boys, or whether they were just that way inclined anyway.

At my prep school, the aforementioned Horris Hill, I I lived amongst some men who, though not paedophiles, clearly had issues with boundaries and whose behaviour made me feel extremely uncomfortable. It was an all-boys school, and there was one teacher who, whether he was sexually active with men his own age or not, took too close an interest in the boys. For instance, he would sit right by our showers after football games and openly look at our naked bodies even though he had no reason to be there (as he was not our sports teacher), let alone looking at us. Sometimes, in full view, he would look straight at our penises. When we had bath time in our dormitories, he would walk through the bathroom, which had a row of baths. By the time we got to the age of 12 or 13, we would all race to foam up our baths as quickly as possible, just to cover up our naked bodies, so he couldn't gaze at us as he walked past. Sometimes, he would actually sit in the bathroom talking to us as he took in the scene. There was one boy who was a little more brazen about how he dried himself off, seemingly oblivious to the adult male who was staring at him as he stood there naked with his towel. The rest of us, however, would be even more coy than usual, making sure we stayed wrapped firmly in our towels.

As young children, unconsciously we are totally switched on to the adults around us, and our nervous systems can spot the ones to be wary of instantly. There were teachers who we were quite happy to have sit in on our bath time and talk to us about football, gossip, or what was on TV. When these teachers were on shower duty in the changing rooms, we'd all breathe sighs of relief. It was clear as day they did not need to be avoided. To grow up in an environment where it feels like there is a distinct lack of safety, and, in this case, an invasion of one's privacy and one's body, is most detrimental.

Worse than just looking, there was a teacher who was an alcoholic, and more evidently a paedophile. Years later, I ran into a fellow student who told me he'd ended up working on a council board who were investigating this very man. He'd left Horris Hill under suspicious circumstances and ended up killing himself.

At Wellington College, I remember getting to the dining room for tea one day, and seeing my friend unusually distressed and shouting at younger boys to get him water. He was usually such a calm and measured individual, so I went up to ask what was wrong. He said he had finished his last A level and had been invited for pizza by a teacher who had plied him with wine, and then started to ask him personal questions about how often he masturbated and how big his willy was. My friend made his excuses and left, but was shaken.

I mention these occasions because the teaching profession was one that unfortunately got a reputation for attracting gay men who were paedophiles. The result was that all gay man got tarred with the same brush. In fact, such was my shame that for years I carried a subconscious feeling that parents were suspicious of me around their children, girl or boy. It is sad that I carried the thought somewhere in my psyche that, because I was gay, people would put me in the same bracket as a child predator.

All the above said, my secret lustings after boys my own age was something that I harboured privately, and although I developed crushes on certain boys and sometimes got to see them in the nude, my thoughts, desires and furtive glances at my peers' naked bodies allowed me to build up a case of utter shame and self-disgust.

I felt like I was being a traitor to my friends, my whole year, to the teachers, to my family and indeed the whole world. I was completely, whole-heartedly wrong and evil. I saw everything through the prejudiced eyes of the world, especially the distaste that my peer group would hold. For young straight boys, the notion of being gay was disgusting, because those young men were exploring their own sexuality, and needed to create and maintain a clear duality between what they were and what they were not.

If someone doesn't like something and it makes them feel weird, their reaction will be dictated by a wider social narrative of what kind of reaction and behaviour is acceptable. Boys in the past have been allowed and guided towards a reaction of outward disgust, projected shaming and emotional and physical abusing towards gay people. The good news is this has changed, with the narrative moving away from merely the sexual attraction and sexual act, and towards that of gay sensibility and love. People are learning to respect the choice of who a person wants to love, even if they don't necessarily agree with it.

Of course, at the age of 16, I was not sitting around musing on the misfortune of young boys being misled by society towards homophobia; I was sitting there thinking I was the devil incarnate, and all these boys would be so repulsed by who I was and the thoughts I had in my head.

So what changed and how did it change? A big step along the road for me was being able to come out publicly, and to reach the 'second stage' of the coming-out process.

I was in my friend's flat in Victoria with one other person. His name was Jon and I'd had a crush on him for the whole summer. I would often drive over to his house in Windsor and we'd go out for a drink. We would talk late into the night, and I became his confidant. When we stayed in Victoria, we would sleep on the same sofa bed, and it felt good to know that Jon was happy for me to be his bedmate. On this particular morning, everyone had gone out, so it was just Jon and me at the flat. Suddenly, I heard whistles and music echoing around the streets. The flat had a balcony, so I went to see what was going on. It was the Gay Pride parade.

Suddenly, around the corner came this whole sea of mostly men, in bright colours, with rainbow flags everywhere and disco tunes blaring out of sound systems. Many of the men were topless, some just in pants. They were all smiling and dancing and singing. I couldn't believe it. From having no visibility in my life of any kind of gay person, there were suddenly thousands passing directly under the balcony I was standing on. I had such an aching urge to join them. I thought perhaps I could sneak down, leave all my friends and join the parade, as if I'd run away and joined the circus. Something stopped me, though, and I was filled with annoyance and self-hatred that I wasn't strong enough to do it. It was years of repression and not feeling safe. It was, however, a key moment in my coming-out process. It showed me that there were other gay men out there who were able to be visible, unashamed and proud to be who they were.

That summer, I started pushing the boundaries as far as I could. I noticed in the tube station in Victoria there was a newsagent that had gay porn mags. It seemed odd that this particular shop had them, as I had never seen them in a newsagent before. It took me a few weeks to build up my courage, but one day I went in and purchased three of these magazines. As I went up to the till, the feeling of dread I had was almost overpowering. I felt as though something awful was going to happen: the shopkeeper would make some comment or judgement, and people in the shop would point and stare at me. Even after buying the magazines, I felt that everyone in the tube station knew what I was up to. It was a mixture of terror and guilt. When I got to the train to take me back to the countryside and to home, I went to the loo and looked through the magazines. I went quickly through them and then squashed them into the bin before I got off the train so that there was no evidence. This became a routine for me. Each time before leaving London, I'd go to this particular newsagent and buy another magazine or two. Then I'd read them on the train, have a wank, and deposit the evidence in the train bin before getting off at my stop.

Slowly, I was finding my own sexuality through these magazines. The interesting thing was that it was done very much in secret and under a veil of guilt and shame, yet it was happening. I found phone numbers in the back of the magazines, and would often go to pay phones and ring them just to hear some super creepy recording of a man speaking about a sexual encounter he'd had. Basically, it was a recording of someone reading a raunchy gay story, and it cost a fortune! I would have to keep on throwing pound coins into the slot to get just a meagre two minutes of story, read by a creepy-sounding American guy.

As time went on, I became more and more frustrated, and I realised I couldn't really hold it in anymore. It was the winter when I went off travelling to Australia for several months, before returning to retake my A levels. Somehow, I knew what I wanted was out there.

CHAPTER FOUR

Finding A Community

We often hear people say 'self-love', but I prefer the term 'self-empathy'. For me, self-love is potentially shaming, while self-empathy is loving in a different way. It's looking at my past with everything I had to endure; all my experiences of pain and sadness. Empathy for oneself, I believe, is the key to healing past shame and trauma. It allows one to really access and understand what has happened in the past. It allows one to observe and offer deep acceptance and validation. *This* is the key. *This* is what is needed, in my opinion, for one to integrate into life and flourish into that butterfly stage.

We are uplifted by empathy because we are listening to our own pain and allowing ourselves to be present for it. Empathy is where we can find a rock from which to view our life. To experience and process years and years of terror and self-loathing, feelings of hopelessness and isolation, we *have* to be present to allow these past experiences to filter out. Self-empathy is the tool by which we can do this. It is the lynchpin to allow stage three of the coming-out process to happen.

I don't really like the phrase 'coming out'. Yes, I can see the positive connotations of bursting out and becoming true to oneself and flourishing, yet there is something about it that seems like some sort of admission. I feel it's now a phrase that is defunct. It's past its sell-by date. People often ask why gay people should have to come out when straight people don't have to come out? For me it ties into that language and narrative of secrecy. The sense that someone was hiding and had been misleading. I would rather use the word declared or stated. To me that feels more empowering; it feels like something that simply *is* rather than coming from the shadows into the light.

On a quick Google search, I discover that the phrase *coming out* was actually taken from the term used for young debutante women in English high society, who when they came of age were paraded in front of the queen at the debutante ball. It meant that a young woman became eligible for courting. In the sixties, gay people would come out into the ball scene in New York. They would come out and be welcomed by their gay family. This explanation seems a lot more positive than my feelings about the phrase. The derivation of the phrase *coming out of the closet,* however, seems to be a mixture of the two phrases *having skeletons in the closet* and *coming out.* It's kind of a mash-up – this one not so positive.

For me, the phrase *coming out* has been tainted in the heteronormative world, be it through written press or spoken word, by the precursor of the word 'admits'. So-and-so 'admits' to being gay, so-and-so comes out, 'admitting' they are gay. For me, this meant that the idea of coming out to family really was the most sickening of things, the primal feeling being one of admission, of holding this dirty secret, and being debased down to my very nature.

*

By the time I was 18, I was at a stage where keeping my sexuality in was becoming more difficult than letting it out, and owning it by declaring it. Still, it was extremely hard for me to take that first step or even to dip my toe into any sort of gay lifestyle or find a community. While I was in-between my A levels and university, living and working in Oxford, I'd sometimes drive down to London at weekends. I'd heard about a gay night called Love Muscle at The Fridge in Brixton, and one night, after leaving the pub with friends, it crossed my mind that I could go. I was due to drive back to Oxford, so I hadn't been drinking, but I ended up sitting in my Mini in a street in Fulham, just stuck, unable to move. I so wanted to drive to Brixton and to go to Love Muscle, but I was simply too scared. I was frozen in the Mini, and upset, wondering how this was ever going to work. How was I ever going to come out if I couldn't even walk into a gay club? I also knew that I was never going to be able to live as a straight person, so there was quite the dilemma going on in that car in Fulham. I wonder now if that's why many young LGBTQ+ people consider suicide … because they just can't see any way forward.

While I was sitting there, unable to move, a Golf GTI pulled up beside me, and when I looked over, I realised that I knew the person driving it. Alex was a cool, straight guy who promoted club nights' sound systems, and the minute I saw him, I felt like I'd been caught out. I was literally just sitting in my car, but I felt as though Alex could read my every thought just by looking at me.

'Hey, are you all right?' he said, clearly noticing my weird demeanour.

'Oh yes, I'm absolutely fine,' I said, launching into performer mode. 'Just looking for my A-Z, you know!'

Driving back to Oxford, I felt so sad. What was I going to do? How was I ever going to make my life work or even be true to myself? It's a memory that's always stayed with me.

Ever more confused, I ended up rekindling a relationship with an old girlfriend. I have to admit, I hadn't been nice to the poor girl, previously dumping her by ignoring her calls, and later seeing her at a party and telling her to 'cheer up!'. I have no idea why she wanted to go out with me again, but she did. I invited her to meet with a plan that we would go out and get pissed, and I could perhaps give the 'straight thing' one more go. Maybe there was even a shag to be had.

The two of us ended up snogging in a club, but by the time we got back to my place, the nerves were kicking in, and I decided that I didn't really want to take things any further. So, instead of the anticipated sex, I made an alternative suggestion.

'Why don't we have a kebab?' I said, thinking that was a good way to delay things.

'A kebab?'

'Yes, let's have a kebab!'

The kebab van was literally one street over, but for some reason, I decided to drive to it. The wrong way down a one-way street. Going the right way up the street, meanwhile, was a police car. Of course, the policemen stopped me and asked had I been drinking. I said I had not. Unfortunately, when they asked me to get out of the car, I fell directly onto the ground, unable to stand, and was promptly arrested. My overriding thought as I was taken away was one of relief that I wasn't going to have to have sex with the poor girl, who was back at the flat, waiting for her kebab.

As it turned out, the policemen were very nice. They kept calling me Jarvis (Cocker) because of the vintage suede jacket I was wearing, while I went on and on, telling them how I was going to be a famous pop star. I also asked for a cell with a view.

I ended up losing my licence for 18 months, but being arrested did get me out of having sex with my old girl-friend, so it wasn't an entirely lose-lose situation.

The idea that I was most definitely gay set in after that, and after a night out in Bristol with some friends, it all came pouring out. I ended up leaving my friends early, very drunk, and crying back at one of their student houses. I believe there was, again, a kebab involved.

Through my tears, I called my old school friend Andrew, sobbing something along the lines of, 'It's back!' Or 'It hasn't gone anywhere!' Even then, I still couldn't bring myself to say the word gay, but Andrew was as wonderfully supportive as ever. My next phone call was my sister, who was also cool with it, although, typically of my family, we just didn't speak about it again for ages afterwards. I was left feeling quite depressed, post that night, but I had little time to dwell on it as I was about to start university in Exeter.

Once at uni, practicality kicked in, and I decided that the only way I was going to be able to be openly gay would be to find a boyfriend. Surely if I fell in love, everything would fall into place. Being in love would matter more than what people might think of me.

One afternoon, I went into the main building of my halls to meet up with Tom and Tim, who were boys I knew from school, and their new friend Adam, who, they informed me, was gay. As I approached the three of them in the hall, it was in a state of teen-movie slow motion. Adam was beautiful, with floppy blond hair, and looked like the sun might actually be shining out of him. He was Leonardo DiCaprio, dressed in Gap. That's it, I thought; this is him. My first instinct, however, was to be mean.

'Oh, I don't want to talk to you; you're gay,' I said, jokingly.

Adam told me later that it was so mean of me to utterly shame him, and I apologised. It was such a clear projection from me and really not a nice thing to do.

After that, I pretty much became obsessed with Adam, and we became really good friends very quickly. We had a similar sense of humour and loved music, plus he was an actor and quite sensitive. He seemed to be as transfixed by me as I was by him, but perhaps for different reasons. Adam had an older brother, who he missed, and I think perhaps I was filling in the gap. As it turned out, Adam wasn't gay, but there was something special about our friendship. It was very intense from both sides, and there were certainly blurred lines, but, of course, I was in love with him.

My love for Adam pushed me into sharing with him that I was gay. I can't remember when I actually told him, but I do remember him checking in with me to make sure I was OK. One weekend, I drove down to London for a friend's twenty-first. At that time, I'd entered a boy band competition on *This Morning* – and was therefore, at this juncture, known as Boy Band Will. People would ask me to sing at their parties when we had all had a few drinks. On this occasion, people were asking me to sing, and, yes, I had already consumed quite a lot of wine.

So, after a speech by the birthday girl's mother, mentioning how her daughter didn't always think she was beautiful, people started chanting for me to sing. In the end, I stood up and sang 'You're So Vain' by Carly Simon. God knows why that particular song popped into my head, but it couldn't have been more inappropriate given the speech that had just been given. I remember my friend's mother giving me a steely look from across the room as I sang, but by that stage I had asked the whole party to join in with the chorus, and was pointing at the birthday girl. 'YOU'RE SO VAIN! I BET YOU THINK THIS SONG IS ABOUT YOU. YOU'RE SOOOOO VAAAIIINNNNN!' It wasn't my proudest moment.

Afterwards, we all ended up going to this awful and expensive club called L'equipe Anglaise in Chelsea. Some of the people I hung out with at that time were very posh, and, I suppose, a lot richer than me, and this was one of those clubs where you paid £200 for a bottle of vodka. I never had that kind of money, and, as was usual, it wasn't a club I would have chosen, but I ended up on the dance floor anyway, because I love to dance.

That night, I ended up running into two friends with whom I'd gone to school. They were both extremely posh, a bit on the conservative side, and rich. One girl, Elloise, was always rather aloof. I thought her cool because she didn't adhere to the convention of being deferential to boys, which afforded her a confident air.

The other school friend I ran into was my friend Percy. There was a notable occasion when Percy came over to our house with his mother one day. Percy had asked me what kind of chocolates my mother would like, so his mother could bring her a sweet gift. I just told him, Flumps, which were marshmallow sweets in a plastic see-through bag that cost about £1. So, when his mother turned up at our house in her very smart Mercedes, she stepped out of the car, and called out to my mother, 'Annabel, I'm afraid I couldn't find any Flumps in Harrods so I bought you some handmade Belgian chocolates.'

My mother whispered to me, 'Why the hell did you tell her I liked Flumps?!', while desperately untying her food-stained apron.

Percy and I went through the horrible prep school experience together, and then ended up both going to Wellington College. He was always a rebel and disliked institution and authority.

That evening, as I staggered through my evening at L'equipe Anglaise, I ran into Percy and sat with him at a table in the middle of the club, paying for drinks off the back of my student loan. In my stupor, I decided to tell him that I was gay. My memory of it is hazy, but I can sort of remember the words and coming out to him and Elloise.

The next morning, I woke up at my friend Serena's house in Victoria. Adam was staying there too, as he'd been out with some other friends the night before. As soon as I was awake, I remembered what I'd done, but hoped to God that it was a dream. A sense of dread froze my body. I began to fall apart in the bed, feeling like I had let something slip that was going to destroy my life. I repeated to myself, 'What have I done? What have I done? What have I done?' It was as if I had opened these floodgates. It wasn't just the statement of my sexuality, but also news of it was going to ricochet around all my old school friends – these people I was still attempting to be friends with; trying to remain one of the lads, and to be accepted. These were the very people who, at school, had signified the reasons why I felt I couldn't come out, and why the world was such a bad and scary place for gay people. They were chauvinistic, loud, hyper-masculine and overtly blokey. I don't blame them, because that was their conditioning. They were conservative, public-school boys, conditioned to be haughty and arrogant, and to think they were better than others. I was fortunate that my parents were different from the norm, which allowed me to have a wider and more accepting view of the world.

Now I had drunkenly told two school friends in a club that I was gay, and all these other people I knew would find out and be disgusted by my sexuality. When I told Adam what had happened, his reaction was so supportive and wonderful.

'This is brilliant,' he said. 'How fantastic!'

Initially, though, I thought it was the worst thing that could have ever happened.

It's crucial to point out that there was another part of me that was happy. I felt like I was ready; ready to tell people and get this pain of holding in the truth of my being gay over with. It was like ripping off a plaster, but, more than that, it was giving a voice to something that I had thought about from the age of six. Something that had kept me in complete confusion, fear and helplessness. Something that I never thought I could ever speak of, or openly live with.

My thoughts until then had always been, how could I live as a 'gay man'? How was it possible? How could I cope with the disdain and the disgust? Now, I'd begun to feel like I could. Maybe I could gain the confidence to not care if it was true, deep down in my soul. There was a definite shift, where the idea of being gay stopped feeling like something that was isolated and segregated and became something that could merge with my very being, allowing me to be an outwardly gay person. The way I thought about my sexuality was slowly changing, and the idea of being gay didn't just mean that I wanked over naked men and fantasised about sleeping with them; it was something that started to seep into my sensibility. I wanted to love as a gay man, and I was ready.

The truth was, even though I'd been paralytically drunk, the two people I'd chosen to tell I was gay were actually the perfect people. Percy was one of the friends I had worried the most about finding out. He was haughty, macho and intimidating. Even as I told him, I thought he might hit me; outraged that I had lied to him for so many years, and had perved on him while we were play-fighting as kids.

As it turned out, I did him a disservice, and for that I now apologise. He didn't thump me in the face; he didn't throw his drink over me. He listened. I can't remember him being emotionally mature and saying all the things that might have been useful, like, 'I validate you, I'm proud of you, I love you', but then again he was never going to be that person. He did, however, accept in his own way. So, as much as I'd woken up that morning, thinking the world was over, I also knew that now it was done, so the only way was up.

From then on was a bit like having a tick list of people to tell … family, brother, girlfriends, friends … The real bump in the road came when I eventually admitted to Adam that I was in love him – that's when everything went tits up! Of course, he couldn't love me back, not in the way I wanted him to. I felt so bad about it, I had to move out of the house. In fact, I was so distraught, I felt I had to stop seeing him altogether because I was so obsessed by him. This would become a pattern for me over the years, and the basis of something I would later discover to be love addiction. I would have a boyfriend, fall deeply in love very quickly, idolise them, break up with them, and then obsess about them for years. And no, we're not talking stalking here, or anything like that: just tortuous obsessing, like a record playing over and over in my mind. That was what it was like for me after my friendship with Adam ended. In fact, it would be some years before we became friends again, during my time on *Pop Idol*. I'm happy to report that we're still friends to this day.

*

I sometimes get frustrated, tracking my journey of coming out over a 30-year period, often wondering why I couldn't have done it quicker. Why didn't I just go off to Soho, aged 18, and meet people or find a friendship group? The answer is, I was so processed and formulated by fear, uncertainty and shame that I was extremely wary of going towards any gay people.

At uni, there was an LGBT society, and I hated them. There was nothing wrong with them, but my gay shame was still in full swing. In fact, there was an element of being 'the only gay in the village' on my part, which added to my disdain. Looking back, I think it's because they were visible: walking around in their platform Buffalo trainers with the odd crop-top. Truth be told, I was probably just envious of how out and proud they were.

I'd come out to a few people by then, and, through word of mouth, most people knew I was gay and I felt accepted. That said, there was the odd bump in the road. One fellow student, who was quite posh and typically public-school, said to me, 'Oh, yes, you're gay now, but you will get married one day, surely!' Jesus Christ, it was like talking to someone's grandfather rather than someone my own age.

Still, it was wonderful to be accepted by the people at university; really beautiful. I'd had this terror, all through my time at public school, that people would find me disgusting, but this wasn't the case here at all. Coming out as gay to my old school friends, however, had been tougher, and in most cases the friendships petered out. At school, I'd been keen to fit in with a group of lads and be just like them, but I wasn't that person. Meeting people like Adam, and another new friend, Tom, at uni changed everything. We were in Footlights together – the university theatre company – and had similar sensibilities. Suddenly the lads I'd been at school with, who wanted to go drinking all the time and were arrogant and chauvinist towards women, seemed a million miles from the person I was or wanted to be.

While I was finding my feet within university grounds, the LGBT society seemed to be living it up, going out to bars and into the wider community in Exeter. Meanwhile, I'd walk past the one gay pub in town, scowling and hissing while secretly desperate to go inside.

I didn't because I was terrified. It was one thing going out to a straight bar with friends, but going to a gay bar was an event, as far as I was concerned. I didn't have any gay friends to go with, so what was I going to do? Sit there drinking on my own? I also wasn't ready to befriend the LGBT society; perhaps through fear of looking a certain way. I didn't want to walk around in Buffalo trainers or a crop-top. It was all a bit confusing.

There were a few bits of sexual interaction, but even they were few and far between. The first came in the form of a bit of naked kissing with a guy one Saturday night. Halfway through, I decided I didn't want to continue, so kicked him out. The thing was, he'd left cocaine on the bedside table, so I called up my friend Amanda, excitedly, at five in the morning.

'I've got some cocaine,' I said.

'Well, get your arse over here!' Amanda replied.

I'd never taken drugs before, and didn't for some years after, but I ended up at her place, having such a great Sunday!

My second encounter was also named Will, so while I was Boy Band Will, he was Stud Will, due to his studded, pierced lip. Things got a bit confusing a year later when I also got a stud and people were thrown into disarray. Maybe we just became 'the gay Wills' post that.

After my first year of university, I drove down to London one day and sat in a café on the corner of Wardour Street, feeling like I was having an out-of-body experience. I was in the middle of Soho, but it felt like I was in a dream; there were openly gay men everywhere. It was summer, so people were sitting outside. There was a waiter at the café who was tall, lithe and blond, wearing a yellow polo shirt. He moved with an assuredness and a knowledge that he was desirable and desired. I couldn't believe it that there was a man who was so beautiful, *and* he was gay. This was a big moment. When I was growing up, especially in my teens, every man I desired was straight. I didn't know any publicly gay men, and came across none at my all-boys' boarding school, so I got used to the sensation that all the people I fancied or thought handsome were straight. I couldn't imagine what sort of chemical equation might produce a man who was really sexy, handsome *and* gay. It just didn't seem possible to me. What are the odds that men who I might fancy would also be homosexuals like me?

Once I got to Soho, I realised the odds were actually rather higher than I expected. There were men every-where. They walked around me, and I felt immersed in a gay story, like I had just jumped into a gay novel. I sat and watched the world pass around me, listening to people's conversation. I couldn't believe that I was in a café surrounded by other gay men. That alone was mind-blowing, exciting, and terrifying. I felt like I was venturing into such an unknown world, but there was no huge feeling of relief, of acceptance or that I belonged. I still felt extremely alien. Everyone was so confident and happy; so public and together. I just felt isolated, stupid and foolish.

At the same time, I was aware that I was taking a step towards 'being gay' because I knew Soho was the gay area of London. What I didn't see was people being beaten up or shouted at. In fact, it was the opposite of that; I sensed joy and togetherness. Even though I didn't necessarily feel it myself, I was aware of it surrounding me.

Eventually, I went to my first gay club with someone from uni who was 'sort of' out, along with his properly out gay friend. We travelled up to London, to G-A-Y at The Astoria, which was one of the biggest gay clubs in Europe. I wasn't at all prepared for the experience. I was 22, and, having never seen anything like it, horrified. There seemed to be a lot of older men with young boys there, and the thought of getting my knob out in the loos was terrifying. I couldn't relate to any of it, and came away feeling deflated.

I did enjoy being in Soho, so a French friend of mine persuaded me to go to Freedom Bar with him and his two sisters. This bar was a lot more mixed than G-A-Y. It was also smaller and seemed a lot less scary. On the small dance floor downstairs, a beautiful young guy was dancing, and the French sisters encouraged me to go buy him a drink. I was shy about it, but they were insistent.

'Go on, just fucking do it,' they said, so off I went.

'Can I buy you a drink?' I asked, shyly.

'Oh, I'm not gay,' the boy said.

I'd chosen the one fucking person in the place who wasn't gay, but when I looked back at my friend's sisters, they were looking at me expectantly. I turned back to the boy.

'Look, my friends are watching me, so can I buy you a drink anyway?'

The guy was quite sweet and accepted the drink gratefully, but that was strike number two as far as my clubbing experiences went.

Once I'd left uni and got my degree, I worked in a bar in Marlborough. There was a gay guy working there who I fancied, and we got it on a couple of times, which meant things were off and rolling as far as boys went. Now we were cooking with gas! However, when I moved to London and started on the musical theatre course at ArtsEd, things changed even more dramatically, with a whole new life unfolding before me.

I moved to a flat in Notting Hill with my friend Mary, not long after the movie *Notting Hill* had come out. To me, it was like living in the midst of the film itself, particularly as Mary's flat had access to the actual garden featured in it. It was an exciting time. I already knew I was down to the final 50 contestants for *Pop Idol,* but I'd decided to keep it a secret and not to tell anyone. As well as that, there were all sorts of new and enlightening things waiting for me at ArtsEd.

When I walked into the men's changing room for the first time, there were four guys doing their make-up in the mirrors, which blew my mind because I was still so naive and shy. A few days after I started, somebody left a note in my locker, saying, '*I think you're really cute*'. It really was another world.

Still, coming from public school, I was quite prim, and the fact that everybody at ArtsEd seemed to be fascinated about whether I was gay or not was something I found tricky. In the student bar one night, somebody asked me outright, 'Are you gay?'

'I don't think that's an appropriate question to ask,' I said, not wanting to be labelled.

The prim exterior cracked once I'd got it on with a couple of guys there; after that I didn't really give a shit what people thought I was.

After I came out, post-*Pop Idol*, I was quite confident and comfortable about being openly gay. The dichotomy was that I wasn't inwardly comfortable with my own sexuality. I didn't have any gay friends, and I didn't go to gay clubs and I wasn't having sex. I guess I did it the other way around to all the other gay pop stars around at the time, who did go out to gay bars and had gay sex but weren't out publicly.

Part of the problem was, I didn't really know what I was supposed to be doing because, let's face it, nobody tells you about gay sex!

Top or bottom? This is the age-old question when approaching gay sex, and something else nobody ever tells you about. These days, versatility seems to be all the rage, but in the past, I've had friends who were obsessed with the distinction.

'Darling, you're either a top or a bottom,' one friend told me. 'And tops cannot go out with other tops!'

To be honest, I've always been slightly fascinated by it.

Before embarking on my first relationship, I remember wondering, how will I know which one I am – top or bottom? I mean, how does it even work? Maybe the answer would lie in the things I masturbated about. Did I imagine someone screwing me in my fantasies, or was I screwing them? Actually, it was never that cut and dried, so that wasn't much help at all.

When I first had sex, it was quite messy, and that affected me for years. Down the line, I've learned that there's a process to anal sex, but the fact is, it *can* be messy sometimes, and that can be scary. I suppose I came to it quite late, at 24, but even then I had to ask my friend the 'ins and outs' of it all, post my first, sticky experience.

'Darling, first you have to get a douche, and then you've got to do this and you've got to do that ... '

I thought, fucking hell! This all sounds a bit difficult.

That first time was quite traumatic for me. I was left feeling dirty and a bit ashamed, as would, I suspect, most of you if you'd shat the bed, aged 24. The upshot of this shame was that I didn't really want to have sex again, or at least not like that. I tried it the other way round, with me being on top, but even then I could have done with someone older and more experienced, explaining it all to me.

My next liaison was with someone who was more top than bottom, but it took me about three months to 'go there', because of my traumatic first encounter. Back then, I didn't know anything about poppers (the nitrate drug sometimes inhaled by gay men during sex). Like a lot of people, I thought that gay men having sex with poppers was just a hedonistic thing, chasing a drug-induced high, but no! Poppers are there to relax you when you're about to have a knob whacked up your bum. Men use poppers to relax their anal sphincter muscle, but no one tells you that.

There is a mechanics to sex that people don't talk about, and, gay or straight, you don't get it taught in schools. They don't tell you that it's not always comfortable for a man or for a woman. They don't talk about things like lubrication, or how to stimulate certain areas of the body. So we don't know what to expect, and end up feeling shame.

A friend of mine shared a story with me. He was 19, and he'd had sex with a guy of about 25, and it was really messy. In this instance, the guy shamed him. He told him he was disgusting and to go and clean himself up. My friend sat in the loo and cried.

The act of sex itself would often re-trigger my shame, because I was engaged in the very thing that was the symbol of being gay: shagging someone of the same sex. Prejudice in wider society meant that there was often little attention paid to the love aspect of homosexuality. People just seemed to focus on the fact that one man was going to put his willy up another man. And that's another thing! Everyone seemed to be obsessed with gay sex and what was going on during it; I think maybe even I was. Whenever I saw a gay couple, I'd wonder who was putting what into whom.

I'm also interested in what restrictions being a top or a bottom put on one's sense of self, for instance, the notion that if I'm the top then I'm the man. I'm macho. I'm not putting out, therefore there's no emotional intimacy. When I did women's studies, women would tell me, 'It's easy for a man to put his penis in a woman's vagina, but it's the woman who is taking something inside of her.' It's the same being a bottom; you're actually taking a part of someone else's body inside you, and the act of entering is very different to the act of receiving.

Unfortunately, that idea of still being 'the man' if you're a top – the aggressive shagger, the dominator – is still out there to a degree. It's certainly more visible with things like Grindr.

I see statements like, *I'm the top, I like to dominate, I don't like kissing, I just want to enter someone,* and I think, Jesus, what's your emotional status? In the past, if you were a bottom, the stereotypical idea was that you're the girl, you're not masculine, you're not a man, you're effeminate, you're weak and emotionally all over the place. Hopefully, that's changing. The fact that more gay men are identifying as versatile is a sign that they don't feel like they have to stick to these assigned roles.

There was a fantastic comment from someone on Grindr a while back. It said something like, '*For people who think that gay men are weak, and for people who think that gay men who bottom are weak, you try taking a cock up your arse! That's the definition of a real man!'*

These days, I don't think I'd be a bottom unless I was in a relationship, because I feel it's more emotionally intimate, and I don't want to do that with someone unless there's a real connection. That said, I believe there's an intimacy in being a top as well. I just wish I'd had all this information about sex when I started out. I could have avoided a lot of pain, and shame!

It really took me about ten years to become a sexually active gay man, and to find a community. It was my boyfriend Julian who helped bring it about. He was a contemporary dancer and slightly more left-of-centre than most of the boys I'd met before. Although athletically built, he wasn't the buff, body-beautiful type, but an indie-kid who wore skinny jeans and was all about the East End: Hoxton, Dalston and Shoreditch. He was also INCREDIBLY sexy and had a good sense of the ridiculous. On my first date with Julian, I said to myself, this probably isn't right, but

I need it right now, and it'll be a hell of a ride! And it was ... It was the most tumultuous relationship, and we had amazing sex. He was the Michael Hutchence to my Kylie. My sexual awakening, and a gateway to discovering a gay scene that I liked, as well as a community that I felt part of.

Julian and I would go out to a great night called Rebel Rebel, run by a friend of ours, Tony Fletcher, who loved Bowie. At Rebel Rebel, they played The Cure or Bowie, or they might play a great R&B track. It wasn't all topless boys, Sugababes remixes and foam parties, which seemed to be what many of the gay clubs were offering at the time; not at all what I enjoyed.

I loved music, so it was great to have finally found a place that, I felt, was me. There was a whole new and alternative gay scene happening around the East End of London, and even though I felt that I wasn't one of the 'cool kids', I liked hanging out with them. Slowly, I started formulating who I was. I'd made new friends, and I'd found a family and these were things I'd had to search hard for, and for a long time.

CHAPTER FIVE

Tea With the Queen

The TV programme *Big Brother* was really a social experiment, and Series 2, in May 2001, was actually momentous. It was the first time, on popular television, we saw a real-life gay man, who wasn't a presenter, comedian or entertainer. Brian Dowling was just a normal flight attendant, going about his business. He was funny, clever, dramatic, occasionally difficult and troubled, but he was kind and sensitive. He won the hearts of the nation. All of us watched *Big Brother* at university, and even though I was out by my third year, and my friends were comfortable with it, none of us, including me, were familiar with gay life, gay people, gay sensibilities or gay romance. Brian provided this for all of us and allowed me and my friends to evolve through his visibility, his appearance on, and ultimate winning of, *Big Brother*. It was significant in educating all of us.

Suddenly, I didn't feel so alone. People were talking about this man, but, importantly, not merely about his sexuality. Mostly, they were simply talking about him as a whole person. His being gay was not always the main topic of conversation. This allowed me to see that a gay man could be accepted as a person; not some kind of monster, or someone who was hugely different and unusual. He was still perhaps viewed as somewhat exotic, and it interested me that in the *Big Brother* house, he became friends with an Asian woman – someone else who was possibly used to life on the perimeter of society. Still, Brian winning *Big Brother* and being accepted gave me real hope. It propelled me forward as I prepared to leave university and meet other gay men, and it encouraged me to think about what it meant *for me* to be a gay man, and where I fitted in with the world. Brian Dowling helped me find my place.

Then, just a few months after Brian's win on *Big Brother*, I found myself on TV every Saturday night in front of millions of people, on the TV talent competition, *Pop Idol.*

In week 12 of the series, the remaining five contestants had to endure a press conference, which was their challenge for that week. At this point, I was aware that people in the media knew I was gay – I'd come out at university, so it wouldn't have been hard to find out anyway. I also knew that no one was going to ask me outright if I was gay. So, when asked who I would like to have a date with, I cryptically and rather masterfully replied, 'I'd like to have tea with the queen!'

I deliberately took the idea of sexual attraction out of the equation. There was nothing anyone could do to criticise my choice or read anything into it. I remember Nicki Chapman, who was one of the judges and a professor of PR, saying to me, 'You couldn't have picked a more perfect answer.' The fact that 'queen' had another connotation made me chuckle internally, and I think the gay journalists who supported me probably chuckled too.

This strategy was something I'd learnt from a very early age. To remain safe, I would give the right answers, while allowing space within my heart to know that I was also being true to myself.

A perfect example would be someone asking me, 'Will, do you think that girl is fit?'

I would say something like, 'Yeah, she always looks fit in a swimming costume.'

My thoughts that a girl looked fit in a swimming costume would be genuine, yet I never went as far as saying I would like to screw her. This allowed me to maintain some self-acceptance. I became known as the boy who was old-fashioned in values, not wildly open about sexual desires, but was also a catch!

I remember one quite laddish friend saying to me: 'You know what, Will, we were all talking, and we reckon you're going to end up with the fittest girlfriend, because you're quiet, you're handsome, you dress well, and you're a bit mysterious.'

I thought, God, if only that were true, it would make life a hell of a lot easier.

Quite why I chose to enter a TV talent show watched by millions is something for my therapist to analyse, but it wasn't the easiest of rides, and my gay shame was, once again, fully in play. Once I'd got over the fear of being 'found out', I began to invalidate my talent, my singing, my style, and the kind of music I enjoyed. Of course I liked listening to soulful women, because I am a poofter! Naturally I would enjoy fashion, because I am gay! I would feel such shame from things that I deeply enjoyed. I hated the fact that I was categorised by the things I liked, and at the same time, I hated myself for liking those things in the first place because they might give people ammunition against me; such was my conditioning from the age of four. The very things that formed my identity became the very things that, I felt, were weapons of war for others to use against me. Not only that; I also used them against myself. Imagine using your very own being and sense of who you are to destroy yourself. That is what I was doing; much of it because I'd grown up in a heteronormative society, which seeks to quash gay identity.

Shame comes from the outside; then percolates, inhabits and spreads from the inside like a disease. Pia Mellody says of disease that it's 'a sense of feeling *dis-ease* in oneself'. This is what shame does. It creates a constant sense of unease with one's very being.

This chapter is difficult for me to write, for several reasons. The first is an overwhelming sense of shame. For I was shamed, ridiculed, and I felt persecuted. It is a strong word, persecuted. I use it because in the case I'm about to mention, I have proof that there was a sustained attack on my character, linked to the fact that I loved men instead of women. I am fortunate that I have evidence of it, but, even now, I sometimes still underplay the gravity of it, falling back on the notion that it might just have been me being sensitive or, perhaps, bitter. The first I definitely am. I was and still am sensitive to the attack that happened. In terms of being bitter, I have done a full inventory of my inner world, and that is not the case. Still, I have been avoiding this chapter because it means facing, head on, an overwhelming force of homophobia laced with cruel humour, passive aggression, and, as far as the print press goes, mixed messages, ridicule and false claims. All this followed by proclamations of the journalist in question and, indeed, the wider press, about apparently having 'no problem' with my sexuality.

It's not just me whose sexuality was being used as a weapon against them, so I have also chosen some examples pertaining to others. I'm loath to print them in this book, as part of me feels I am soiling the pages by including such bile and toxicity. Yet, I am purposefully surrounding it with a message of love and acceptance, in the knowledge that, ultimately, love and acceptance conquers vindictive and purposeful disdain and prejudice.

The first interesting case happened in October 2009, when Stephen Gately of the hugely successful band, Boyzone, died in his sleep at his holiday home in Mallorca. The article, written by a journalist whose name I can't even mention because it fills me with such anger, disgust and fear, appeared in the *Daily Mail* and is the textbook example of how oily and obsequious prejudice and gay shaming can be. Never quite going full-out in its ridicule of gay men, but where the overall feeling, post reading it, is one of dirtiness. One feels dirty reading it. The journalist is dirty and their output is dirty. What's so interesting is that the Stephen Gately article I speak of, and the one on myself, were both written by women, which somehow makes it worse. For me, bigotry from a male is more cut and dried. When a man is unable to deal with his own sexual nature or his fears, he projects his self-loathing and shame outwards onto a minority. It's seen time and time again. Women are not generally as threatened by gay men as their straight male counterparts, so I find it harder to understand. The female journalists who wrote this article remind me of the character in *Harry Potter*, Dolores Umbridge, played in the films by Imelda Staunton. Cleverly, she is portrayed as the archetypal *Daily Mail* journalist; the perfect face of 'home counties' prejudice and cruelty. There was also a teacher at Wellington College who had the same air. I was in her form when I was 13, and was terrified of her. We called her The Chainsaw. The Chainsaw had set, permed hair, and always wore a jacket with matching skirt and sensible shoes. As far as I was concerned, she was bordering on evil: her face didn't betray an ounce of kindness. The Chainsaw went against any sense I had of women being maternal or nurturing, but I guess that was my prejudice. I mean, why was I so narrow-minded as to think that women could *only* be kind and sensitive? Being only 13 at the time, I guess I can forgive myself for that assumption, but even in my twenties, I seemed to be surrounded by women who were kind, had control of their emotional world, and were certainly less threatened by gay men.

I don't wish to dissect the *Mail* article about Stephen Gately, because I would never in a million years choose to engage in a dialogue with the type of journalist who would write it. They attack their prey like snakes, always seeming to come out on top, while making the injured parties look like oversensitive, over-protective citizens who should just grow a backbone and not be so reactive. This is a great example of a journalist using the development of gay rights as a weapon against them. There were something like 30,000 complaints made to the PCC (Press Complaints Commission) due to this article, which I believe was some sort of record at the time, but I don't recall there being a retraction or apology printed in the paper. If there were any, it would have probably been tiny and lost on page 32.

The headline of the article was, 'A strange, lonely and troubling death'. In it, the hack reports that the causes of death were reported as natural – an undetected heart defect, as it turned out. Her suspected version of events is somewhat darker; she says that the circumstances around Stephen's death were 'more than a little sleazy', implying that it was his hedonistic, gay lifestyle that was the undoing of him. She points out that Stephen and his partner had gone home with a young Bulgarian guy, post-clubbing, suggesting that 'a game of canasta with 25-year-old Georgi Dochev was not what was on the cards'. This leads her to the conclusion that the circumstances around Gately's death 'strikes another blow to the happy-ever-after myth of civil partnerships'. She then berates gay activists who call for tolerance and understanding about same-sex marriage.

When reading this article, which is far more sinister than just the few bits I've recounted, I'm reminded that it comes from a newspaper that represents the worst of middle England. Year after year, decade after decade, this paper has been responsible for headline after headline that has spread prejudicial dogma in a terrifyingly subtle yet cruel way. Dolores in *Harry Potter* would inflict the punishment of giving lines to her students, but rather than writing them out on paper, they would have to carve the words into their skin. Dolores did all this with a smile on her face, which draws a terrifyingly accurate parallel with the kind of journalism that I, and so many people, have witnessed over the years at the hands of these merciless journalists, supposedly writing truth for their readers. Writer Charlie Brooker wrote a brilliant dissection of this homophobic diatribe, labelling it a gratuitous piece of gay-bashing.

The attitude that LGBTQ+ people are oversensitive about this kind of thing is still seen in certain TV commentators. We love to hate them, and heads of networks are more than happy to have them on their channels for this very reason. These are the people who use terms like 'snowflake generation' to dismiss anyone who disagrees, feels offended, or takes a stand against them, and to bolster the validity of their comments and views. It's often said that 'you can't say anything nowadays without offending *someone*'. Well, here are my thoughts on that argument:

if I am ever concerned about offending someone, I simply ask beforehand. If I have potentially offended someone, I will say that I am sorry for their feelings of offence. This does not mean that I have to apologise for what I have said; I am merely apologising for the fact that they are feeling a certain way. I respect the right of anyone to have their opinions and their views; however, I do not have to respect the manner in which those views are sometimes put across.

The other thing is, anyone who enters a debate or certain topic without curiosity is being closed-minded. If I am unsure about something, I try to remind myself to be curious about it rather than afraid. I made a decision a while ago never to enter a debate or confrontation with someone who immediately comes at me, or others, from a ridiculing and judgemental standpoint. It's a waste of my time, and I simply do not feel safe around this kind of person. They scare me because they are not interested in any level of truly empathetic intellectual debate. In fact, to engage with them simply puts more wind in their sails. A person who throws a punch and doesn't make contact with anything uses up all their energy, often falling flat on their face. So let them! There are, however, times when people should stand up for themselves and their community and the article on Stephen Gately's death was one of them.

After winning *Pop Idol*, I was yet to tell people in the press, and therefore wider society, that I was a gay man. In those days, there was no social media. I couldn't pre-empt any salacious press articles by simply sending a quick tweet or posting a video. Social media has given control back to many celebrities, in that they can set and control the narrative rather than the mainstream press and media.

At the beginning of my career, the narrative and stories were guided, as much as possible, by my PR team. The relationship between certain elements of the press and the PR team often became fractured and resentful. Sometimes, negative stories were written about me, purely because there was wider beef with the press team and a particular tabloid. On one occasion, my PR team decided that I should not do a particular article in a particular newspaper, so the editor 'punished' me by printing a piece filled with character assassination. I actually can't really remember everything it said, but there were some very choice bits, including one that said I had demanded pink towels on a tour. Incidentally, on the tour in question, I was incredibly depressed and uncontained, which spilled over into me behaving like a twat and rather unpleasantly. I did not, however, ask for pink towels, and I think we can all do the maths as to why that particular colour was chosen. It's actually a great example of homophobia being used, but in a very underhand and subliminal manner. How could simply saying I demanded pink towels be homophobic? Well, since the whole thing is made up anyway, why not choose the colour blue? No. The newspaper wanted this story to portray 'the queen': a dramatic and bitchy pop star. A drama queen who is demanding and entirely unpleasant. Actually, I *was* being fairly unpleasant; not because I was gay, but because I was being a dick and couldn't contain my emotional turmoil at the time.

About two months after winning the show, a horrible and upsetting piece was written about me in the *Mail on Sunday*. In the build-up to this piece, I had gone through my own journey in terms of being a gay contestant within the growing fame and pressure of being on a Saturday-night TV talent competition, which had exploded in terms of popularity and therefore attention; to give an example, the show started with an audience of around 900,000 and ended with an audience of 14 million watching the final. That is around one fifth of the entire British population watching the show.

I knew that just by going on the show, if I was to progress and ultimately become a pop star, my sexuality would become 'a thing' within all that. When the competition got down to just ten remaining contestants, we were told at a meeting, by the PR team, to be aware that things might come up in the press that weren't always positive news items, and that the tabloids would be looking for 'dirt' on all of us, especially as the competition reached its climax. The team also said that it was a good idea to tell family and friends to not speak to the press. It was at this meeting that I said that I was gay, but it certainly wasn't a big deal with the PR team or the other contestants. Post that, as we got nearer to the final, I was sitting in the auditorium of the TV studio, talking to a couple of new people in the press team, who, at one point, asked me to not speak about my sexuality publicly. It was put to me that, as we were so close to the end of the series, it would be a shame to let *that* be the overriding news story rather than a more positive one.

I saw the truth in this, but at the same time told them both, quite forthrightly, that I had not gone through all of the difficulties of coming out to now deny who I was. I had spent years pretending to be someone else, and I was now proud of myself for having come out, and having taken on that fight, as it were. It appalled me that people were even suggesting that I should not be true to myself.

Such was the climate at this time that no one would talk about their sexuality within the pop world. It was an unspoken rule. We saw it with George Michael, until he was effectively outed by the LAPD. People in the industry and the press knew that Jon from S Club 7 was gay, as well as Stephen Gately, and Mark from Westlife. No one would print it or ask the question, though, and certainly no promotional poster would announce it. It wasn't until later that it was deemed OK for pop stars to come out. For me, there was no question as to whether I'd be open about my sexuality or not. I would be. The agreement the PR team and I eventually came to, and the way I was approaching the issue anyhow, was that if someone asked me the question, I would not sit there and lie. This, I imagine, led to a massive panic behind the scenes, with PR representatives trying to vet who would and who wouldn't ask the question, because the tabloids all knew already anyway! It wasn't long before the PR team found out which publication was indeed going to ask the question, and it was panic stations a go-go!

It was the last week of the show, and there were two contestants left: Gareth Gates and me. At the beginning of the week, it was decided that we should each go aboard our own individual tour buses and 'campaign' up and down the country. It was a genius idea, and as a politics student I could see the intelligence behind it. *Pop Idol* even ended up being debated in the House of Commons, because of the phenomenal success of the show, and consequently, all sections of the media wanted to interview us: from tabloids to evening chat shows to political editors. We were in hot demand. The PR strategy had been incredible and the team behind it was inventive, authentic and, most importantly, made it fun. I had the best time during that week. There were some things I'm sure that I've forgotten about, but my overriding memory is that it was seriously busy but there was a lot of joy and laughter.

We used the top deck of the buses for interviews; there was a small sitting room at the front of the bus, where each journalist got 15 minutes of one-on-one time with me. The interviews were mostly tabloid press, and the one we all thought was going to prove trouble-some was the *Daily Mirror*. They had a celebrity page, written by three women called the '3am Girls'. Initially, I'd thought this meant that it was hosted by three prostitutes, which I thought brilliant, so I was a bit disappointed to discover that the '3am' bit meant that the girls stayed out late at all the celebrity parties to get all the best gossip. It's hysterical writing about this now, because it all seems so petty and ridiculous; so far removed from anything of any importance in life. Which was more important: 9/11 or the 3am Girls; Syria or the

3am girls: the ever-decreasing tiger numbers, hurtling towards extinction ... or the 3am Girls? At the time, however, they did become an important thing in my life. I was constantly being told what the fucking 3am Girls were writing about me on any given day! God knows why people felt the need to tell me, but I had to be told. Not only that, my PR team expected me to have an answer to every story that came out anywhere, and would continually call me for comment.

On one occasion, a go-go dancer from a bar in Soho told the press I had slept with him. He said the we had spent the night together and that I wore camouflage boxer shorts. I didn't, but for some reason, even to this day, I am most offended by the suggestion I wore camouflage boxer shorts. It was a strange life, because not only did I have no privacy from the press, but also none from my PR team. I always wondered who made up the rule that said that the press could ask my PR team anything, and they would, in turn, have to ask me. It gives an idea of the level of power that the press held back then. This was pre-mainstream internet, so the tabloids wielded their power and dug deep for salacious stories. Of course, we all know where this ended up, which was the phone hacking scandal.

Anyway, there I was on my bus, awaiting the arrival of the 3am Girls, or at least one of them. I'd been told three times that *this* would be the woman who would ask if I was gay, and three times I'd said I would reply truthfully. It was suggested that my PR person might, as soon as she heard the words leave the journalist's lips, whip me away in an instant. However, the interview progressed, and, as we got to the end, the journalist actually looked rather apologetic. She told me that she had to ask the next question because she had been forced to by her editor. Quick as a flash, I was removed from the room. It was as if there had been an attempted assassination and my bodyguard was rushing me out of the danger zone: 'GET HIM OUT! NOW!! GO, GO, GO!!!'

I jest, but I was grateful to the person, Kat, who oversaw my final week there. She knew the whole thing was bollocks and felt bad for even having to give a shit. As with any form of bribery or shaming, if we turn around to these people and say 'I don't feel ashamed and I don't care what people think' it takes the wind out of their sails. They have nothing to barter with, and no power. It was interesting that with my sexuality at that time, it was seen as something that the press had 'found out'.

The narrative at the time was still that being gay was secretive, and therefore, by association, shameful and wrong. As mentioned previously, even when people would speak honestly about their sexuality, the headlines would be: 'so-and-so *admits* they are gay', the emphasis being on the notion that it's some sort of confession; the outing of a dirty secret. Tell the truth and stop trying to fool the public.

Some people would have it that I *was* fooling the public. And what about all the young girls who followed me? Wasn't I giving them false hope or wronging them in some way? This notion was prevalent in pop, especially in boy bands. If a boy band member was gay, the press line was that they were keeping it from their fans in order to manipulate and use them. Of course, this was bollocks, but also in line with the attitude of record labels.

Their line was mostly that a gay person should not come out and talk about their sexuality. Avoid the questions about personal matters, so as not to risk alienating your fan base, and, ultimately losing income for the record company, management etc. Within the music industry, it came down to finances. People thought that what they were doing was best for business, and best for their clients. They didn't ever consider what the consequences might be for a person, being persuaded to repress a basic and central part of their very being.

After *Pop Idol*, I did come out publicly. It was carefully planned. I met with a litigation lawyer named Gerrard Tyrrell, who worked with a firm called Harbottle & Lewis. He was, and is, a calm, intelligent and measured man; well-spoken, always well-dressed, and you just know that he is a good dad. We got on from the get-go, possibly in part because I was middle-class and had been to public school, as had had Gerrard. He worked with the royals, and my brother was going out with Rose Windsor at the time, so we had some connection and, I guess, a lot in common. What is crucial, though, is that Gerrard was not stuffy and not a snob. I felt safe with him because he was gentle, honest and protective toward me. Fleet Street feared him, and well they should. Years later, it was Gerrard who aided many well-known people in the phone hacking scandal, including myself.

Together, Gerrard, the team from Henry's House PR company and I hatched a plan that we felt was right and authentic and true to me. We decided to do an interview for an article in a broadsheet, deliberately setting out the agenda on a more intellectual level than that of a tabloid newspaper. Before it was due to happen, which was within a month or so of me winning the show, I stayed in close contact with Gerrard because so many stories about me were cropping up. I was convinced that Gerrard was in the Territorial Army, because every time I spoke to him at the weekend, he was up a mountain. I also bumped into him at Buckingham Palace after the queen's golden jubilee – the man got everywhere.

'You're either a spy or in the SAS,' I said.

He laughed and then moved on, no doubt to chat to one of his many clients in the room. I note that to this day he has not denied he's in the SAS.

About a week before our article, speculative stories started surfacing in the tabloids. I think I'm correct in saying that it was actually libellous to 'out' someone in the media, so, instead, various factions of the press were dancing rather unpleasantly around the issue. They had probably got wind of what Gerrard and I were planning, so turned the heat up accordingly.

There were several more phone calls between me, in my friend's Notting Hill flat, and Gerrard – probably climbing through some cargo net in the hills of Cumbria – and, before I knew it, it was the Sunday before my planned public coming out. That day, the *Mail on Sunday* ran the aforementioned article, which was read to me, word for word, by one of my press officers. I can remember exactly where I was standing to this day: in the doorway of the sitting room, half in and half out of the hallway, in my friend Claire's house in Battersea. Claire was a girl from university, who I'd lived with in my final year, and we were true, true friends. The night before, her partner Hugh and I had taken turns driving a tuk-tuk back from Soho to Battersea. We'd put the driver in the back with Claire, and then asked him in for a party. Anyway, Michelle from Henry's House told me on the phone that, legally, she had to read it to me. I'm not sure why that was the case, but I acquiesced, and as I stood there at Claire's, planted between the sitting room and the hallway, I listened to quite the nastiest and vilest thing that someone, in all my 22 years, had ever directed toward me. It literally took my breath away. Despite trying to tell myself that it didn't matter and that it was tomorrow's chip paper etc, it hit me hard. So hard, in fact, that I have only read this article once since that day, after I emailed Gerrard and asked him if he happened to have a copy on file. He did, but went further, sourcing other pieces from the past that serve to highlight the homophobic climate of the time, and how an out gay man, who happened to be in the public eye, was treated.

When Gerrard sent me the article, I found it incredibly hard to read, because it is so triggering of the shame and self-hate drummed up by this kind of bile. The heading was, *'So Will he last? Wealthy, a degree in politics and whispers about his sexuality ... Will Young is the unlikeliest of pop stars. As he heads for No.1, will his grin be enough to win him long-term stardom?* Catherine Ostler, who wrote the article – aside from being insulting about my physical appearance, upbringing and talent – suggested that I'd no doubt soon be 'whooping it up in The Ivy at one of Elton John and his lover's David Furnish's intimate little all-star soirees'. She added a quote, supposedly from one of my colleagues at Exeter, who says I pranced around, dressed like one of the characters from *Fame*, making everything larger than life. She talked of a 'colourful rumour (is) now doing the rounds', in which a group of my friends at Wellington College were involved in the bullying and homosexual intimidation of younger boys. And that's just a small part of it.

After Michelle had read out the piece to me over the phone that morning, I asked her whether we should sue the paper. I remember the conclusion was that to do that so early in my career was a huge risk, as I would not only alienate one paper, but it would get the backs of other tabloids up, setting them on attack mode towards me as well. I could just imagine it: '*Who does Will think he is?*';

or, '*Look how quickly he has turned against the press who have always been so supportive.*'

The truth was, I wanted a career and I believed in my ability. I wasn't arrogant – far from it – yet I was fiercely protective of my talent, and I would have been hugely disappointed if my career had ended before it had begun. I had a deep drive to succeed, but I also wanted to prove everyone wrong. *Pop Idol* was not seen as credible by much of the music industry or, indeed, other pop artists, so I was not necessarily a popular or revered artist coming into the music arena.

I was handed instant fame and instant success, and I had the fastest-selling single of all time for a debut male artist. My success didn't happen normally. I hadn't paid my dues, as far as people like Paul McCartney, the Gallagher brothers, George Michael and Boy George, to name but a few, thought. It broke my heart that some of these people were so anti the show, and therefore, by default, anti-me. In my head, I had five years to carve out a career, so I had to very carefully weigh up whether I wanted to jeopardise all that potential because of an article written by a bigot for a bigoted paper. In the end, I chose my career over the chance of being massacred, and, rather than look for remuneration and compensation for such slander, I bowed out, saying nothing.

To this day, it's one of my biggest regrets. I feel cowardly and disappointed that I chose to ignore it, and yet I also recognise that I probably didn't have a choice at the time. My thinking was that, if I took on the paper and my career folded because of it, then the journalist, and the newspaper, would have won.

It wasn't just the power of the media that stopped me suing the paper; it was also the fact that homophobia was not even seen as a big deal. It really wasn't. Back then, it would have been seen as petty and overly sensitive to take on any paper over homophobic content. There was little around, either legally or in society at large, to support gay people. No legal rights, no marriage, nothing occurring within schools, and hardly any 'out' public figures. I hadn't even publicly come out yet, so I had no platform of support to stand on.

I had no idea what the reaction would be when I came out, but to come out and immediately be suing papers left, right and centre would allow the press to carve out an image of me as a militant, and a radical; undesirable and disruptive. It would, without a doubt, have destroyed my career.

After that horrific article, the *Mail on Sunday* stayed true to form, saying they were going to 'out me' in their next edition. So, after more phone calls to Gerrard – who was probably on a rock face on Ben Nevis – we decided to abort the broadsheet plan and get the *News of the World* on side. We would do a story with them that ran on the Saturday, therefore scuppering the *Mail on Sunday*'s plans to get the scoop, and the glory. It worked – those fuckers must have been furious!

That Sunday, I was booked to do a writing session with the pop writer, Cathy Dennis. She had just penned 'Can't Get You Out of My Head' for Kylie Minogue, and went on to write 'Toxic' for Britney Spears, 'I Kissed a Girl' for Katy Perry, and many others. It was the last thing I wanted to do, but my management had decided the best thing was to keep me busy.

A driver rang my doorbell and said he was ready for me, and that there were a few photographers at the front door. I got myself ready and decided to empty the bins on the way outside, as it was rubbish day the following morning. I walked down from the fourth to the ground floor, opening the door to the Georgian block of flats I lived in, and there in front of me, at the end of the big front steps, were about 40 photographers. *How do they always manage to find out where famous people live?* It was like the scene from *Notting Hill,* where Julia Roberts is caught in Hugh Grant's house after nude pictures of her are leaked. Some photographers outside my building had bought their own mini-stepladders, so they were able to see over the scrum. It was crazy and terrifying. My favourite thing about the whole ordeal was that I was taking the rubbish out. The headline the next day was: '*Will Young Comes Out ... With the Rubbish!*'

Maybe subconsciously I brought the rubbish out with me to try to normalise the situation and show that I was less concerned with being gay than I was with emptying the bins. I remember shopping in Tesco on Brompton Road – one of my favourite places to be – that evening, after a day of unsuccessful writing with Cathy, and feeling a sudden shiver of a panic attack. I suddenly felt as though everyone knew my business and all about my sexuality. I no longer felt sheltered, knowing everyone now knew I was attracted to men. I felt naked and vulnerable. My physical safety was now compromised and I was completely exposed. As I scanned my chickpeas and mayonnaise (such a nutritious meal), I realised that things would never be the same again.

Despite being terrified on occasions, I was also stuck between a rock and a hard place. I wanted to be true to myself, yet I also wanted to have a long and successful career, and finding that balance was very difficult. When I re-read my coming out statement from my *News of the World* piece, I'm sad that I felt I had to downplay the idea that I was a campaigner or an activist. It's true – I wasn't at that time because I wasn't yet truly comfortable in my sexuality or ready to look outwards to wider society – but back then I knew I had to come across as acceptable, friendly, and absolutely no challenge to anyone: 'Don't worry, I won't offend you. I sleep with men, but I will never talk about blow jobs, so your own sexuality and sense of self doesn't have to be threatened.'

I did have a point to make, which was that being gay wasn't a big deal, and in some way, I suppose that was my form of activism back then. The more I downplayed being gay, the more other people might see that it was OK and that gay people aren't a threat. Perhaps that might move the conversation along. The problem was that I was stunting my own growth as a gay man, and this was encouraged by those around me. I was advised to always avoid any questions involving me being gay, so the issue wouldn't take over a whole interview, whether it be on radio, TV or in print.

I understood that what I offered, as a 22-year-old openly gay male pop star, was a new and unique viewpoint for journalists. Not only did they want to know what it was like to be a talent show winner, but also what my thoughts and feelings were on being gay. To be honest, unlike now, I didn't actually have masses of thoughts on it. Still, I think I did myself a disservice in some ways, and certainly feel that I would have benefited from having someone to guide me as a young gay man within the industry. I found myself in such a paradox. I was openly gay, yet advised to not push my sexuality. At the time, I saw the value in this line of thinking, and therefore diminished part of myself for profit, and to ensure that I held onto my career. I don't think I could have done anything differently. What saddens me, and I have since found peace with it, is that I often did myself an injustice. I remember doing a TV show on Channel 4 called *T4*. It was a morning programme that ran across Sunday morning from around 9am to midday. The presenter was the lovely Vernon Kay, who had been a model and was very funny. I was doing a number of clips and songs for their Christmas special, and at one point I sat on Vernon's knee, while he was dressed as Father Christmas. He asked me who I wanted to kiss under the mistletoe and I clammed up instantly, knowing that I shouldn't mention anyone male.

'I would like to kiss Beverley Knight,' I said.

Beverley Knight was a soul pop singer who I, indeed, greatly admired, but certainly did not want to kiss! It was slightly soul-destroying having to lie in those moments, despite believing that it was for the 'greater good' of my career.

When starting my podcast, *Homo Sapiens*, with my friend Chris, I freely recounted tales from my pop days, and as I began to reflect on those times, a growing sense of anger occurred. This encouraged me to meet up with Michelle from my old PR team, to express how I felt. It was eating me up, and I needed to get it out. Talking to her, I felt instantly better; she was extremely respectful about my feelings back then, and of my feelings throughout my career. We were all trying to do the best we could, and we had to operate within the restrictive circles that existed back then – the power of the media, where wider society was at with gay people in the UK, and even what the legal system gave us recourse to do and not do.

It was a very different time, but amidst all the times when I would feel berated and attacked, things happened that made my heart sing with the acceptance and love I felt from complete strangers.

CHAPTER SIX

Ancient and Modern Stereotypes and Homophobia

I recall, back in 2002, walking down Portobello Road, where there was an enormous poster for my first single, 'Evergreen'. It was common for record companies then to put up a poster near the pop star's home. As I walked past the poster, some builders on a site pointed up at the poster and called out to me.

'Way-hey, Will! Go on, my son! You're a handsome bastard, aren't you? If I was gay, I'd have a go!'

I mean, it was just amazing. As so often throughout my life, the type of person I had thought would be the most terrifying was actually the most surprising. The obvious lad, for example; the builder. I have found that these guys often have the biggest hearts, and don't give a shit about what you do or who you are; they just like people who are nice and down to earth. Still, as a gay man, and being a publicly gay man, I found myself putting people into categories based on whether I thought I would be safe or not. I became my own walking Mori poll for homophobia. I was, however, time and again, beautifully surprised by people from different ages, genders, religions or ethnic backgrounds. It was a constant source of joy and still is.

It saddens me that I found myself placing people into boxes and making assessments. I would call them 'risk assessments' rather than judgements, as I wasn't looking to make moral assessments on people. It was more about whether I could get away with being publicly gay around these people. How young were they? What class? What culture? Were they posh? Were they businessmen? Having this radar was imperative. Ask most gay or queer people, and they will tell you that they have a radar, which is constantly on, scanning for danger. Being famous meant I had a double-radar, because I was always subconsciously looking around to see where a phone might be shoved in my face, or a piece of paper and a pen, or rush of ten people. This was my life. It was neither good nor bad; it just was what it was. Sometimes, my assessments about people were wrong, and I was happy to be proved wrong; yet often they were right, and I was desperately sad and hurt.

Having gone to public school, I'd spent a lot of my late teens in Chelsea with all the other rich privileged public-school boys from Eton and Harrow and Radley. It was a stomping ground I was familiar with, and I felt a certain affinity with many of the posh people who lived there. However, when I was walking by the Bluebird restaurant one day, someone driving by shouted at me in a posh voice:

'Bumboy!'

I immediately felt exposed, ashamed and embarrassed. It's strange; the silence that occurs after an insult has been hurled can be a silence that creates a sort of complicity. No one says anything; people walk on, and the words hang in the air, filling the space as if they'd been shouted by the whole street instead of just one person.

The street takes on the cry: 'You're a bumboy! You're not welcome here.'

I was devastated. I felt like even the area I was most familiar with in London had let me down. Somebody who I might have even played at rugby had abused me, and I felt disgusting; almost as if in exile. The public nature of it was even more humiliating and terrifying, but didn't stop there.

In South Kensington, not far from the King's Road, I went into a sandwich shop where I had been going for around four years. I was playing at Wembley that night with the other nine finalists from *Pop Idol*, and I wanted to grab a panini to go. I got my driver, in his blacked-out Mercedes, to stop outside the café (one other thing I'd learnt very quickly was that the blacked-out Mercedes was one of the few places I actually felt safe and not stared at) and walked into the busy café to queue for my panini. While I was waiting, a girl of around 17 came up to me and shoved her phone into my face, demanding I spoke to her mother. I very politely declined but sent my best to her mum. Once I'd got my lunch, I turned to walk out, but as I passed the girl she said, 'Is it because I'm a *girl* that you wouldn't speak to my mum, Will?'

She said it loud enough for the whole café to hear, and I couldn't believe it. I couldn't comprehend someone that age would be so hurtful, unpleasant and outwardly homophobic. I couldn't even believe that a young girl would actually think like that. I am, however, proud of what I did next.

I turned at the door and said loudly, 'No! It's because you're FUCKING RUDE!'

Everyone stared at the girl and I walked out rather pleased with my reply. I was also shaken and deeply angry. It wasn't to stop there though. I was off to Wembley to do the final day of the *Pop Idol* tour, which was being filmed. It was the first show since I had publicly come out. The support of everyone in the *Pop Idol* camp was palpable. All the other contestants were wonderful and we were like a family.

The first half of the show was fun and went really well. Midway through the second half, there was a moment each night when some of us would gather around a sofa under the stage, which was then lifted up into the middle of the stage. As we walked up to take our places around the sofa that night, I noticed that someone had written FAGGOTS in chalk on the wall. It wasn't just me who was gay either; there was another young guy called Korben. He looked crestfallen, and I was devastated for him, feeling extremely protective. I was furious and, in front of the whole crew and the tour manager, loudly demanded a towel and some water. The tour manager tried to stop me from doing it, but I brushed him gently aside and doused the towel in water, washing the foul word off the wall.

I looked around. I didn't know who'd written it. Our tour manager, Bill, a tough Scottish man, was furious that anyone would dare write something like that on his watch, and I certainly wouldn't have fucked with him! I got the words off just in time, before we all rose up together to face our audience for the upcoming number, feeling strong and united. We never did find out who'd written it.

Things like this continued to happen, and somehow, I managed to remain resolute. I'm not sure where I got the courage or countenance to be so tough, because in other ways I was completely broken and had very low self-esteem. I think perhaps from my upbringing, and from doing politics at university, I managed to have a strong sense of not being bullied. I have always detested bullies and bullying was something I wouldn't stand for. Looking back, though, it can be scary. I've had people threatening to stab me and I once had someone shouting 'queer' and 'faggot' at me from a Vauxhall Nova outside a pub in Hampstead. Although on that occasion, I just shouted 'faggot' back at them, so they just got confused and drove off looking rather dejected. Someone also once rang my hotel room late at night to homophobically abuse me. At the same time, I constantly came across people who would surprise me with their warmth and open-mindedness.

Around the same time as the Stephen Gately article came out around his death, a DJ on the BBC Radio 1 breakfast show, Chris Moyles, decided to embark on a rampage of homophobia against me – on my birthday no less. It was something that left me aghast, especially as he and I were on friendly terms. My manager at the time, Caroline, heard it, and was truly angered. She could not believe the language that was being used against one of her clients.

I have never heard the show or read the transcript until now, but I managed to find it through Gerrard, who has supplied me with not only the audio and transcript of the show, but also the replies from the BBC, who weren't exactly falling over themselves to apologise.

It's important now that I make clear I am not using this as an example purely to relive some personal gripe against Chris Moyles, the BBC, or Radio 1. That said, I did feel that, back then, Radio 1 was a bit of a hotbed for anti-gay sentiment, despite them having a gay DJ, Scott Mills. Scott was never, to my knowledge, vocal about his sexuality on air at that time, but I have always been a supporter and fan, and interviewed him for an edition of *Attitude* when I was guest editor.

I'm sure the audio version of the piece has a blatant feel, due to the words being used. The written word also has a toxicity and can cut deep; however, there is something flagrant about live spoken words. They cannot so readily be changed, or explained away as being taken 'out of context'. Chris Moyles presented the Breakfast Show, probably attracting the most listeners at that time of day across the whole of the UK, so the homophobia against me was beamed through people's radios in their cars, their homes, their workplaces, and to their ears, as they got ready for, or travelled to, work, school, or college. Here, my sexuality was something to be mocked and laughed at, which is without question encouraging homophobia.

Announcing my birthday, he put on a silly, overly camp voice, spouting things like, *'Hello, Will Young here. Ooh! Look at the muck in here.'* And *'It's my birthday, gonna wear a new dress tonight. And I smell nice. I've had a shower and shaved my legs. Going out later, might go to Nob-ooh for my dinner.'* And *'I like to wear a silly hat; I get camper by the hour. I'm Will Young and I'm gay. Did you know I was gay? I hid it for a while. But now I'm out, I'm outer than you would believe.'*

What Chris Moyles did that morning on BBC Radio 1 was reinforce the idea of gay men as laughable creatures, who are oddities and camp, prancing about in dresses, wearing make-up – effectively, anything other than the stereotypical macho normal man. This idea of gay men being somehow fodder for jokes is not something that has slipped away, unfortunately. As recent as 2019, the TV car show, *The Grand Tour,* had Jeremy Clarkson in what was described as a 'hairdresser's car'. He laughably wore a pink shirt, and played 'It's Raining Men' in the car, while the other presenter, Richard Hammond, spoke of wearing arseless chaps. Absolutely hysterical! Of course, I'm *sure* Jeremy 'isn't homophobic in the slightest' and I would imagine has 'loads of gay friends'.

It wasn't just the presenters who were at fault either. It was, most notably, the show's producers, who decided to lead with this stereotyped gay theme as one of the stories for the show. They chose it, they format-ted and initiated it, and yet I'm sure they don't consider themselves homophobic, merely funny. Also, let us not forget the complicity of Amazon in allowing this show to air, even though I'm sure they see themselves as a very forward-thinking diverse company and have a very good internal 'LGBT' network. Let's imagine that ethnic minorities were being stereotyped and made fun of on this show. I don't even want to consider that would be the case, and neither, I'm sure, would Chris Moyles or the producers of *The Grand Tour*. Yet, for some reason, gay people were, and unfortunately still sometimes are, fair game.

This goes wider than radio and TV. Films, over the years, especially laddish films like *The Hangover*, would have actors making fun of two men being gay. The idea that one of the straight men has become gay is made to seem like total hilarity. Actor and writer Seth Rogen has consistently perpetuated homophobia through his movies, and has recently apologised for doing so. But why did he and others not see at the time how offensive these parodies and jokes were? After all, it wasn't all that long ago. The key thing in all of these cases is that there are gay people watching these films in the cinema, while others around them are laughing. It's the same with radio and TV. These stereotypes compound the shame and self-hatred that gay people can often feel, and the examples I've given show just how little corporations, producers, presenters and actors have, in the past, cared about the effect their 'creative' decisions have on others.

The Chris Moyles debacle is interesting because it was happening under the umbrella of the BBC, a body governed by central government and paid for by the taxpayers. They, if anyone, should be expected to have been more responsible and responsive to diversity, and serving all the people who paid their licence fee, not just some of them.

At the time of broadcast, the BBC were resistant about providing a transcript of the show and the language that occurred on it. One could not imagine it happening these days, and to me, it shows how there was an ability to hit back against issues being raised such as homophobia at that time. What is also notable was the lack of complaints at the time. Perhaps Chris was preaching to the choir, or perhaps the fact it was meant to be humorous meant that people didn't really think there was anything wrong with what he said. For me, it demonstrates how low on the agenda the idea of gay rights and equality was. The action taken by the broadcaster was minimal. Thankfully, though, things were starting to change.

With civil partnerships and the emergence of equal rights for the LGBT+ community, the teaching of issues like gay rights, equality and lifestyles was seen in many more schools and colleges. LGBTQ+ pop stars, actors and sportspeople began to become more prominent. It stopped being such a scoop that someone was anything other than heterosexual. The prevention of the use of the word 'gay' as a derogatory term in broadcasting was upheld, and people were called out on their bigotry and prejudices more and more. TV shows and films became more diverse, and more and more LGBT+ stories appeared in mainstream broadcasting. Visibility was bigger, better and more prominent. Mental health amongst the LGBT+ community was addressed more, and transgender rights were brought to the fore. The notion of what it was, and is, to be queer has arisen in the last few years to greater prominence. Gender norms and identity are discussed frequently, with a movement that is continuing to grow. It is an inescapable and undeniable force of evolution; a wave that has continued to roll along. Sometimes, these waves gently break on sand, and other times they smash into rocks of resistance. The path of improvement is never straight and simple, but the determination is undeniable. Legal structuring is now in place, so as LGBTQ+ citizens of the UK, we are protected by a framework and precedents, which have been formed to help us fight prejudice, and keep us from harm by those who perpetuate that prejudice. It's fair to say that a sea change has occurred in the past few years, not only in wider society . . . but also in myself.

Over the years, I've heard straight men who enjoy my music say things like, 'I like your music, I mean, I'm not gay, and the boys in the office make fun of me.'

Or a straight woman might say, 'My husband likes your music; sometimes I think he must be gay.'

Neither of these sentences make me feel particularly fantastic about myself. I think because I was not so much the norm in terms of being a pop star who was open from the start about who he'd fall in love with, it presented men with a definite dichotomy. If you like Will Young then you must be gay or at least a bit odd. For a long time, this would reinforce the gay shame I held inside and I would find myself agreeing with these comments. It was an example of how we are all stereotyped and put into boxes, and I think the people who can suffer the most are straight men. In fact, as I've said before, the people who are exposed to the most homophobia are straight men: constantly ribbed about being gay in the locker room, the workplace or in their own home.

It seems that the kind of pop star you like is used as an indicator of the kind of identity you must have, but stereotyping doesn't stop there. It can be anything: the car you drive; where you live; the clothes you wear. It's all an illusion created by society to keep us in our separate places. Once we realise that we can do and be whoever we want, the world is the most liberating place. If I want to, I can wear a skirt and still be masculine. If we want to, we can listen to Radio 4 and still be the coolest, hippest person on the planet! We are controlled by the limitations that are put on us from the very beginning of our lives. Wear the colour blue if you are a boy, pink if you're a girl. I even heard on a radio breakfast show yesterday that the man doing the travel was expecting a baby. The presenter asked if he knew the sex yet, and the man said he didn't, so the presenter replied, 'Well, only gender-neutral colours for now then.'

This implied and reinforced that there are colours that aren't gender-neutral, and I was surprised to hear the presenter say these words. If I was having a child and someone bought me a pink Babygro – for the child, of course! – I wouldn't care if I then had a boy or a girl. The baby wouldn't give a shit, I can assure you. This is an example of us actually putting our hang-ups and limitations directly onto our children – starting at the infant stage, for God's sake! In fact, as the radio show highlighted, it starts before the bloody child is even born, so what hope have they got?

We have to work on our stuff and free ourselves from these rules that have been created and passed down but that mean absolutely nothing, only serving to limit our true power and ability to be whoever we want to be; not what others expect us to be.

I know this now, but I'm sad to admit that once I was 'publicly gay', post-*Pop Idol,* I found myself shying away from the areas of life where I felt I didn't belong. I stopped going to watch rugby matches. I noticed that when I did go, as an out gay man, I felt extremely vulnerable and self-conscious. I had a dialogue constantly running in my head. I felt I could no longer 'masquerade' as a straight man going to watch a rugby international at Twickenham; instead, I felt open to ridicule and public disgust. Bear in mind, this was back in 2002 when LGBTQ+ people were still considered fair game. There was no embracing of the LGBTQ+ community. They were still very much seen as misfits who were tolerated. But it was just that – tolerance, not acceptance.

The truth is, even now, as a gay man, I have to think about where I feel I belong, and where I might feel unwelcome or even unsafe. Not long ago, my brother Rupert and I were on our way to a gig when we saw a couple – two men – holding hands. Both of us remarked, not only how lovely it was, but how brave. It made me remember how scary it had been for me, holding hands in public with a partner for the first time. A few things came to mind. Firstly, if I see a heterosexual couple holding hands, I don't think, 'Oh, they're heterosexual!' It doesn't enter my head. Whereas, with two people of the same sex, the notion of their sexuality is there, and it registers as something good, and, yes, something brave. Holding hands in public is such an open, gentle and physical declaration of being in love, but for gay people there is always going to be a safety aspect. If I'm holding hands with a man in view of everyone I happen to walk past, I can't control how each person will be affected by that.

I was wandering through the East End about fourteen years ago, holding hands with my then boyfriend, Julian, and we had people shouting at us. Someone actually threatened to stab us. We ended up taking shelter in Les Trois Garçons, which is a restaurant owned and run by a trio of gay men. Further back than that, my first boyfriend, Jude, and I were holding hands as he walked me to the BBC in White City one day. As we approached a group of teenagers on the street, we both consciously let go of one another; it was instinctual. The memory of those occasions makes me feel sad and reminds me that even now, in certain situations, I have to be on alert. We all have to be on alert, because we might not be safe. We might get attacked or beaten up. It's happening even now, as in the case of the lesbian couple who were attacked and left battered and bloody on a bus in Camden Town, in 2019.

The sad truth is, some people are still offended, incensed or indeed disgusted by the sight of same-sex couples displaying affection in public, and it's something most gay people take for granted and learn to live with. I was on my way home in a cab once, having been set up on a date with a guy who, I'd been told by several people, was an exceptional kisser. In the back seat of the taxi from Soho, I happily discovered that everything I'd been told was true. Yes, he was a fantastic kisser, and I made a mental note to call the friend who'd set us up the next day, to report my findings. Now, I say we were kissing in the back seat and that's what I mean. We weren't having sex or anything approaching it; it was a snog. Still, the taxi driver stopped his cab and kicked us out on Oxford Street, telling us we were disgusting. I didn't choose to fight it. Perhaps I could have, but what would have been the point? Yes, we were upset about it, but in some ways, we just accepted it. I kissed someone in the street on a recent date, but even then, I was conscious of the risks, and, although the thought may have been fleeting, it was there.

Travelling can also be a minefield. In some places I've visited, men are advised not to hold hands, which immediately puts one on edge. It's something gay men and women always have to consider. For instance, I probably wouldn't think twice about holding a partner's hand around the pool at the Four Seasons in LA, but in the majority of hotels I've been to, that wouldn't be the case. Who would look twice at a heterosexual couple having a quick snog in the pool? Two men, on the other hand ...

In a London hotel, my boyfriend Jesse and I were messing about in a giant Jacuzzi – more of a pool really – with me holding him in the water like a baby learning to swim. I don't think we even kissed and we certainly weren't snogging, because I don't think that appropriate in a hotel Jacuzzi, whoever the hell you are. I remember this big Russian guy watching us, and it was clear that he didn't like what he saw. Not long after, the manager of the hotel arrived to say that there had been a complaint about us, and could we stop what we were doing.

I lost my shit.

'You would not be coming down here if we were a straight couple,' I told him. 'This is blatant homophobia, and you've made the wrong decision.'

Not only were we doing something completely inno-cent, but this hotel was in the centre of London, a stone's throw away from Trafalgar Square, where Gay Pride was happening on that very day.

It's sad that as a 41-year-old man, I still feel I have to consider so many things before taking a simple action. I have to analyse the people around me, then decide if I still want to take the action, and whether it's safe to do so, and then consider whether I'm even within my rights to do it. All this within a few seconds.

It makes it hard to live authentically because one is sometimes – whether it be consciously or unconsciously – pandering to someone else's standards of acceptability. It means that same-sex couples often have to look for safe spaces to be themselves. So however out and proud we might be, it's not exactly true and authentic living.

Happily, things have got better in many places, and people are more and more accepting, but for me, that consciousness around safety is something that will always be there. It's a way of living that I know will never change for me. I just have to work at it, and decide, on a day-to-day basis, how brave I want to be.

I've sometimes discovered bravery and visibility in the strangest of places. When I bought my house in Cornwall, which is in the middle of nowhere, on Bodmin Moor, I was surprised to discover two gay men running the local pub. I thought, Wow! These are the people who are really on the front line. I've found a certain amount of safety, living in London, but things can sometimes be trickier for same-sex couples in more remote areas, because they tend to stand out more in smaller communities.

One night at the house, I was hosting a hen do for my friend, Claire, where we'd all dressed as different characters. Claire was dressed in a repulsive dress that I'd found for her, and I was dressed as a granny. On that same night, the local pub was holding some sort of anniversary celebration in a marquee on the moor. How brilliant, I thought. We can all go and join their party later on in the evening.

When we arrived at the marquee, a cry went up, 'The 'ens are 'ere! The 'ens are 'ere!' Clearly, they'd been expecting us. In fact, about ten years later, I was told that the hens' arrival had been met with much approval from the local men.

'Ooh, look at that one, she's fit!' the postman had said, seeing one girl. 'And that one, she's nice!'

On seeing me, he'd remarked, 'I'm not sure about that one; she's a bit of a boot!'

All in all, it turned out to be an interesting night. I ended up getting up on stage with a local band, while wearing a dress, and singing a song. Later, I got propositioned by a handsome young farmer.

'Come on, Will!' he said. 'Let's have a bit of a quick kiss!'

'I can't,' I told him. 'I have a boyfriend.'

As well as that, one of the regulars felt compelled to tell me that she'd found her son in the hayloft with another boy from the village. I remember thinking, what's going on? Is there a pink cloud over Bodmin Moor I don't know about?

It was a great evening, and a lovely example of me being as open as I wanted to be in an unexpected environment. And let's face it, I'm an openly gay famous person, so I couldn't have hidden my sexuality even if I'd wanted to. As it turned out, I was completely accepted in that small community, and I think the fact that two openly gay men ran the local pub was a massive help.

While I was outside chopping wood one day – my favourite pastime – I spotted a group of men walking along the footpath that went through the land around my house, so went to have a chat with them.

They turned out to be the Cornwall Gay Men's Walking Group, which was quite a surprise to me. They were a wonderful group of guys, who were doing something other than clubbing – just walking. I loved the normality of it, and it struck me how important this kind of group is. This was how people found community, especially outside the big cities.

*

Thinking about country life, and being gay in a village, brings to mind *The Archers* – the longest-running radio drama, possibly in the world, I think.

It revolves around Ambridge, a made-up town in the countryside, somewhere, I think, in the Midlands, and is largely about the farming community. It runs twice a day from Monday to Friday, the lunchtime episode being a repeat of the evening before. On Sunday there is *The Archers* omnibus where you get a blissful 75 minutes of Ambridge's latest sagas. Highlights include potato rot, the positive and negatives of herbal leys and my personal favourite, the village cake competition. I adore Lynda Snell; she's snobby and a busybody, and likes to talk about Chaucer and use Latin. She is – again that elusive word – 'camp'; I find it hard to put into words quite how she is camp, but she is!

My parents and I now have a WhatsApp group where we discuss what's going on with *The Archers*. Kate is one of the characters who often gets it in the neck; she's spoilt and really annoying, and my mother can be quite vitriolic about her. In fact, my mother is also on the Facebook page for *The Archers* and can sometimes get into quite heated conversations about various storylines.

There is a gay couple – Ian and Adam. Ian is a chef at the well-to-do restaurant and spa and Adam is a farmer. Adam and Ian are possibly the dullest gay couple I have ever come across in fiction or in real life. In fact, I think they are just the dullest couple full stop. Adam in particular is seriously pessimistic and has a way of speaking where every sentence has to end in a downward inflection. I would like to be clever and say that my dislike of them comes from some intrinsic gay shame in myself or inane jealousy of how this fictional couple are together, and yet I am single. I don't think it is, though. I think they are just shit boring. They are however having a baby with Lexi, one of the Polish cleaners, as a surrogate, using one of their sperms; so although I jest, *The Archers*, which is probably marketed to an audience of age 60 years plus, is actually broaching modern-day topics and reaching across middle England in its own rural way.

CHAPTER SEVEN

Breaking the Patterns of Addiction

I was rebirthed once. It wasn't something I expected, but it did lead to a very bizarre few hours which, ultimately, allowed me to process a big chunk of residual gay shame.

The queen, after Princess Diana's death, said in her Christmas speech that 1992 had been an '*annus horribilis*'. Well, mine came in 2012. It's odd recounting this, because it feels like old ground now, and besides that, it really isn't all that interesting. How many more times can one read about someone who's had a breakdown and got through it? Blah, blah, blah! We all know that movie and how it ends. It did happen, though; I had a proper breakdown. However, life didn't immediately go from 0 to

100 on the breakdown scale. I wasn't drinking coffee one minute and then in the foetal position the next. It was a slow unravelling.

I first realised it was happening when I couldn't get out of bed, which was very unusual for me. I had recently got a Border terrier puppy, who I'd named Esme, who would sit and watch me in the mornings, and I would think, 'why is she judging me?' That was one of my finer moments of therapy actually, saying to my therapist, 'Lois, I think my dog is judging me.' I'm sure it was then that she diagnosed me with PTSD. I mean, I'm not sure if judgemental animal projection is in the list of symptoms, but who knows?

Incidentally, one of my other fantastical moments of therapy gold was going to see a shaman and, halfway through the regression, wondering if I might be Jesus. Do with that information what you will.

The next big thing, alongside not getting up, was not being able to eat anything for days, and then just managing to make it to the kitchen to collect dry cereal, and taking it back to bed. It was like student life, but with none of the fun. Poor Esme just sat in bed with me while I stuffed cereal into my face. The other thing I noticed was that whether I was eating loads of food or none, I was dropping weight and was looking super skinny. There is one video I shot during this time, and when I see myself now, I look too skinny and have a sort of 'lollipop' head.

The final thing happened on an evening when I was due to take Esme out for her little walk before bed. It was getting harder and harder for me to leave the house, and this particular evening, I do not exaggerate when I say that I walked half bent over with terror, with Esme on her lead. At that time, I lived in a gorgeous house on a gorgeous square, and my lap around that square took me about 15 minutes. It was excruciatingly painful in such a weird way, and this was when the penny dropped that I was, indeed, having a breakdown.

It was something I had only heard about, with someone occasionally whispering, 'Oh, he had a breakdown a few years ago ...' about someone. The inference seemed to be that the person had never quite been the same since.

I can attest to that, but not in a shameful manner. I have, indeed, never been the same since, and although so much has changed for the better, life has, at times, been extremely difficult. Being able to say to people that I was having a breakdown was actually quite amazing, though, probably because I was actually in the midst of one! You hear people talk of heading for a breakdown or having had a breakdown, but not often of being IN one. I was in it big time, which I found to be quite an interesting conversation opener at parties. Not that I actually went to many parties; I couldn't leave the house. Looking back, I sort of wish I'd been able to do more TV shows and be completely honest at that time, because somehow, I was still managing to work.

'And welcome to the show, Will Young.'

'Thank you so much for having me on.'

'So, Will, you're looking great and very svelte; how are you doing?'

'I'm great, thank you, and currently going through an incredible breakdown: not eating, staying in bed and taking my dog for walks by crawling along the pavement.'

'Er ... Will Young, everybody.'

I started going to 12-step meetings, which were actually very useful. To be honest, I hadn't even thought of myself as an addict of any sort. I mean, I wasn't on the street. I wasn't staying in my house for weeks on end taking drugs, but there were a few things that led me to face up to what were, I came to realise, very clear addictions.

I never really used porn when I was in a relationship, so when I did, it often came out of loneliness. I would watch it at night, alone in bed, which, I imagine, a lot of people do. However, my period of masturbating over porn at night got longer and longer as the hit I was getting from it diminished. So, a five-minute wank was turning into an hour-long marathon.

Not that I have any problem with masturbation. It can alter your mood for the better and help settle your nervous system, but I often felt a sense of loss and abandonment afterwards, because I was lonely, and what I really wanted was connection. Eventually, I was watching porn in the loo on my phone at a department store, or silently in the back of a cab (not wanking, I hasten to add) but I still didn't think I was being triggered into a state by it, until in 2012

I went on an experiential course where we all had to stand around a fire, write something down on paper, say it aloud to the assembled group, and then throw the paper into the fire. It was saying the words aloud that helped me realise that my porn habit *was* addictive, and how ashamed of it I was. I was expunging my shame by sharing it.

Some of the course wasn't quite as helpful. Like the time I had to lie on a plastic mat and imagine I was dead and about to be buried by my family, voicing all the reasons they might have been disappointed by my death. I never quite saw the point of that, and also it was raining outside. I remember thinking, what the fuck is this all about, as I listened to people all around me, vocalising from their plastic mats.

Aside from porn, there were other addictions. Love addiction, for example. This can be a difficult topic to grasp. It's when we obsess about our potential or real partner. We live without any boundaries; we are desperate to do anything to gain validation. Often, if we're a love addict, we'll be attracted to someone who is a love avoidant and unable to give us what we emotionally need. Love avoidance also falls under the love addict category, in that a person can be drawn constantly to relationships, yet will withdraw, because, emotionally, they are unable to give their partner what they want. Both love addicts and love avoidants can be driven by a deep fear of abandonment. The addict clinging to the other due to terror that they will leave, the avoidant seeing being left as inevitable, so they create a scenario to make them feel like they're in control.

Often in relationships, we can yo-yo between love addicts and love avoidants, attracting the opposite, depending on what energy we are giving out.

I did a love addiction course in Arizona, which, ironically, started on Valentine's Day, and it wasn't terribly glamorous. I stayed in the kind of motel where murderers go to wash the blood off their hands, and every night I ended up going to the McDonald's drive-through for my dinner. On my third appearance at the drive-through, I arrived to find the entire staff peering at me through the window, giggling. As it turned out, they couldn't believe my accent and thought I was Hugh Grant. I corrected them, telling them that I was, in fact, royal.

The joy continued when I caught pubic lice from the bed sheets at the motel and ended up at a clinic, which was set to cost $900 for treatment. However, I managed to swerve that particular expense after telling the doctor I was a musician, and him asking me if I knew the band Elbow, who he loved. I lied and told him I did, so he let me off paying.

Love addiction is nuanced, and for a while I didn't really get it. A love addict is someone who might meet someone and immediately think, *Yes! He or she is the one! They will fill this void in me! They will take away my shame and the pain of abandonment!* It's immediate and very heightened, but ultimately those kinds of relationships rarely work, because they – *we* – are often attracted to the kind of person who will, again, abandon us. These days, I walk away when I feel that kind of rush, which is a high rather than a warm feeling in your tummy. I try to steer clear of acting on that kind of impulse. It is a very difficult pattern to break, and one I am still working on.

I was addicted to shopping, I used alcohol and cigarettes as a mood alterer, I was addicted to buying houses (a rarer disease, yet I had the means!), I bought loads of cars. I still have the rush of shopping inside me, and it flares up on occasion. The reason we have addictions is to take away the everyday pain we are living with.

Interestingly, despite my long list of addictions, I never felt I was a sex addict, although, for me, apps like Grindr haven't always been the healthiest of things. Grindr is a fascinating hunting ground that, in my opinion, is rarely healthy. I have, on occasion, had some great adult sexual experiences, where I just wanted the physical contact of sex. Even then, there was probably a yearning, and emotional hole that needed filling. The profiles on Grindr I find most fascinating are the ones that simply show a rippling torso, yet the accompanying biogs say that they are looking for an adult, long-term relationship. There are a lot of those. It is a sign, in my opinion, of how worthwhile the person thinks they are, and there is a clear paradox. The person looking for love perhaps wants marriage, yet thinks the way to get it is to display his best asset, which is a gym-toned body.

A while back, a friend asked me why I didn't have a boyfriend. As it happened, there was no particular reason, while his reason for not having one took me aback slightly.

'I want to be in a monogamous relationship,' he said. 'Everyone I meet doesn't want that.'

'I find that odd,' I said. 'You're saying you don't meet anyone that wants to be in an exclusive couple?'

'No, I don't,' he says. 'They all want to be open or just to sleep around.'

He was 32 years old, and in his experience, everyone in in the gay community wanted open relationships so they could sleep around.

I think the perception of gay men is often that they are sexual beings who just want to shag the whole time. Some people can't even grasp the idea of two gay men being friends without fucking. We're all just fucking, all the time. It's a constant orgy. There's also the idea that many men just aren't able to keep their knobs in their pants, but that's not just gay men, that's all men. If straight men could get away with hooking up with the ease that gay men do, I'm sure they would.

The truth is, I have friends who are in open relation-ships and they are very happy about it. In fact, they are thriving, and it's lovely to see. Still, hearing about this particular friend's experience surprised me and made me a little sad. I'm sure there are many gay men in monog-amous relationships, but are they in a minority? Perhaps I thought that marriage might have solidified the idea of an exclusive gay couple, and that two men might choose to just sleep with each other and no one else.

I continued to work through all my addictions in the 12-step programme, and I managed to get to a much deeper level of trauma than I'd expected. At the time, I'd just started in the musical *Cabaret* at the Savoy Theatre in London, but halfway through the run, my body gave up and went into full-on protective mode. For around six weeks, I thought I was actually going insane. I lost all sense of where I was and who people were. Emotionally, I could not connect to anything. It was like I had become a robot. I couldn't see my face in the mirror.

One day, I went for lunch with my manager, Faye, in the same restaurant in the same area I had been going for 12 years, but I didn't really have any clue who she was. I started 'falling away from the table', as if I were next to myself, watching the conversation between the two of us. I had no emotional connection whatsoever to Faye. It was extremely difficult to describe to people and at first I wondered if it might be the new medication I was taking.

After weeks arguing with my psychiatrist – who at one stage said, 'Fuck you! I'm the expert,' which was incredible and, within the context, brilliant and totally cool – I finally found, through the power of Google, that my symptoms matched completely that of various forms of disassociation: called depersonalisation and derealisation. Interestingly, since going public about these two disassociate conditions, some people close to me experiencing the same thing have opened up to me, telling me that they also had no idea what was wrong with them.

Once the conditions really took hold, I had to go into residential treatment in Oxford, Khiron House. I knew Oxford well and felt comfortable there, and Khiron House was near to the university parks. I'd lived in Oxford before, while retaking my A levels, and I'd worked on the high street, so as much as it was a relief to go into the house for treatment, it was also nice to be back in such a wonderful place. This is not to say that my time in treatment was a holiday camp. It wasn't.

I arrived in the house having already done some group therapy work. Plus, having done the 12-step programme and some work on boundaries, I felt well equipped to handle what was to come. I was fortunate enough to have my own room at the top of the house. There were around eight of us residing there, and, if I remember correctly, there was only one other man. Our day consisted of group therapy in the morning, a break, and then either mindfulness or a lecture before lunch. After that, we would either have art therapy or Tai Chi, before another group session, which was followed by yoga. Group therapy was one of the most, if not *the* most important factor in my recovery. To sit and be open about what was truly going on, and to hear others who were feeling similar things and telling similar stories, was hugely calming. It allowed me to see that I was not defective in some way, odd or peculiar, and also that I wasn't going mad. I quickly became friends with a couple of people, but got on well with everybody.

Art therapy was one of my favourite things, even though when I first started it, I was presented with some moulding clay and asked to 'sculpt' my feelings. I recall sitting there on the floor of the basement room that looked out onto the garden thinking, 'how the fuck did I end up here? I am 35 years old, and I am being asked to mould clay. The last time I did this was when I was five.' I remember it clearly because I'd tried to eat the clay and had to go to the doctors. By the end of art therapy, however, I was fully engrossed in it, and my defining piece was created during my final week, when I'd decided to do an art installation in the compost heap. I painted my face and hung my coloured socks all around a chestnut tree that stood above the compost heap. I had become fully ensconced in the garden, and it was a huge source of comfort to be able to mow the lawn, clear the leaves and create new flower-beds. Tracey Emin I was not, but I like to think that my work, which I titled 'Compost Corner', still lives in infamy in that small corner of an Oxford garden.

Everyone in the place had their own little foibles and characteristics. Mine was walking around coughing the whole time; something I had developed since getting ill. Somatically, it probably represented the repression of or attempt to deal with emotions that were flooding through me. When I was younger, I'd had various tics, as well as a persistent sniff that I still get to this day. It's a wonder people didn't think I was some sort of cocaine fiend.

Another resident, who I shall call Barbara, was constantly making cups of tea, yet after about three sips would put them down and forget where they were in the house. She would also insist on stirring her brews with any biro or pen she could find. Once a day, we would have to go on 'mug hunts' around the house to find out where she had left her various refreshments, and along with the recovered mugs, we would find the various pens and biros we had been using throughout the day to take notes or whatever.

Barbara was one of the characters who, outside the walls of the house, would have been labelled crazy or mentally ill. Inside the house, she was just Barbara, and she had some shit to deal with. We were all, in fact, just a bunch of people in a lot of pain, terrified and at our wits' ends, trying to make sense of how we had ended up there. Nobody was judged, and nobody was better or worse than anyone else. In this respect, it was the perfect household. That said, Barbara was certainly one of the more fascinating residents. She masterfully avoided doing any cooking, and would occasionally go into other residents' cupboards and take little items of food. A few biscuits here, some croissants there. She was like a little thieving squirrel. One day, I was especially looking forward to the Magnum I had saved for that evening. On discovering that my section of the freezer was bare, I immediately walked over to Barbara, who was reclining innocently on the sofa.

'I know you've eaten my last double chocolate Magnum, Barbara.'

'William, I am outraged at this very accusation,' she said. 'Be assured, I shall be taking it up with the highest authorities. Outraged, I am.'

'Barbara, I know you've eaten it,' I said. 'But out of interest where would you be taking this matter if you hadn't?'

'Well, I will, of course, be taking it to the Vatican,' Barbara said.

Barbara was a staunch Catholic, when it suited her. She would call me a sinner for being gay, and a pointless celebrity who was spoilt and unnecessary.

One afternoon, she decided to give herself a makeover and appeared late to 'check in' at group. It was Friday, and she'd decided to put on make-up and curl her hair to look as if she was going out for the evening. In she walked with a sort of of half-permed and half-straightened hairdo. She had mountains of pink blusher on her cheeks, unblended, red lipstick that was sort of smeared around her lips, and heavy mascara on her eyes. This gave her a look of what could only be described as a scary Russian doll. As she sat down and waited for everyone else to check in – which just meant taking a minute to say how they were feeling that day – she became more and more fidgety, clearly dying for people to comment on her new look. No one said anything, so she kept on craning her neck around, and sticking out her face to show, in silence, the transform-ation she had created. As she caught a person's eye, she'd give a knowing smile and a nod as if to say, 'I know, right? I'm a knockout, aren't I?'

In group, we would be encouraged to ask for some 'time' if we wanted to talk about stuff that was going on for us or resolve conflicts. We would ask a person if they were open for feedback, and if the person said they were, then we would create a safe dialogue around whatever was going on. Time could be used for expressing something that resonated in oneself when another resident shared, or could be used to air grievances within the house. On the day of Barbara's makeover, I immediately asked for time.

'Barbara, are you open for feedback?' I asked.

Barbara was over the moon at this request. 'William, I am indeed; speak on.'

'Barbara,' I said, 'when I see your face and what you've done, I'm reminded of a French harlot in sixteenth-century Paris, who also steals ice creams and forgets where she has left her various customers around the city.'

Barbara squirmed with delight in her chair. 'William, are you open to feedback?'

'I am, Barbara.'

'William,' she said, without any hint of irony or sarcasm, 'thank you. That is the *exact* look that I was going for!'

Describing, analysing and investigating where my gay shame was rooted and how it developed was only part of my journey. I noticed, after reading a fantastic book called *Healing the Shame That Binds You* by John Bradshaw, that there were many other symptoms of shame that I exhibited.

Perfectionism – I was fixated on making everything I did at work perfect. If I sang a note I wasn't happy with, I would dissect it afterwards. It wasn't just that I wanted work to be perfect, but I also wanted to be a 'perfect' person. The best friend, the best son, the best pop star. The problem with perfectionism is that the ultimate conclusion is we aren't good enough. As soon as we are in a perfectionist cycle we set ourselves up for a fall. It is an unattainable goal and therefore is a tool we use to berate ourselves and reaffirm our core belief that we're not good enough.

Comparing – Along with perfectionism, I found myself constantly comparing myself to others. This infiltrated my entire life. In work I would compare myself, in friendships I would conclude that others were doing better than me, and it ripped through my relationships, really fucking me up. I even compared myself with everyday people on the street: their clothes are better than mine; I should be driving that car, not the crap car I have; I should be living in this street rather than the one I live on. It was constant, and it was again a cycle that would ultimately end up with me feeling shit and not good enough. When we enter the comparison game, the end result is that we are often left feeling defective, or that our lives are failing. There is however another nuanced conclusion to the comparison game, which is that we go 'one up' on others. It is the alternative option to going 'one down' and yet it is still a sign that we carry core shame. Our self-esteem is so low and lacking that we compare ourselves against others and conclude that we are much better than they are: better looking than them, or that we have a much better car or job or new suit. It is something I used to do, and always felt so ashamed of. As soon as I read John Bradshaw, and also Pia Mellody's work, I realised why I always went into these cycles of comparison. Whether we get a quick fix from going 'one up', or the kidney punch of a reaffirming 'one down', the result is ultimately the same: a dead-end road of shame and self-hate. We enter the comparison game because we have deep wounds.

Fixing – I LOVED being the fixer. The person who would solve the problems of others. I was very good at it. It was something that allowed me to feel wanted, useful and worthwhile. If I was solving people's problems, listening to their hardships or their relationship woes, I was someone who was worth having around. I'm still very good at it, only now I make a huge effort to do it in a non-co-de-pendent way. My co-dependence was that if I wasn't fixing other people and making them happy, I could not be happy. I relied entirely on other people's lives. In fact, I often wouldn't allow people to just sit with their feelings and find their own path. I denied people their realties so I could shift mine.

Anger – I never thought I had anger issues, but I did. I would often internalise anger so in close relationships, I would strop, withdraw and isolate. Sometimes, I would explode, but this was mostly within a work environment. I never really understood why I did it, because it never felt truly like me. Something would just take over. I think this can often happen in a relationship, where we find ourselves becoming someone we don't even recognise. This is a sure sign that 'stuff' from our past is hijacking our present reality.

Inability to have adult relationships – relationships were not my forte. When I got into a relationship, I became obsessive in my thinking. Now, a lot of this was down to core abandonment, which was something separate from my gay shame. I would rely too much on a sexual relationship, rather than connecting on a deeper and more loving level. The intensity of sex would seem like love;

however, it was merely a plaster over a lack of connection. Sometimes, we confuse intense sex for a true connection with someone. For me, it's a litmus test of a connection that is based on abandonment and shame. Many therapists say that if two people get together who both have abandonment issues, and will, at some point, abandon each other physically and emotionally, the sex is so intense because it is based on a yearning from both parties. Incidentally, this doesn't mean sex cannot be intense, yet true, loving sex in a functional adult relationship feels very different. My relationships would generally have a honeymoon period of about a month before my insecurities would creep in. My modus operandi was to compare myself and always come off worse. I wasn't gay enough, slim enough, cool enough, I didn't have as interesting friends; it could be anything. It was debilitating and really destroyed me while I was in a relationship.

Body dysmorphia/obsession – body obsession is a sign of emotional pain. In the gay world it's glaringly noticeable on various apps, and in real life, of course, people can be obsessed with how they look. We may think we are too thin or too fat, not muscly enough or too muscly. I think I had body dysmorphia for years, thinking I was too fat. Now I look back at pictures, I really was quite the little Twink – with a very sporty figure! A Twink-Jock, perhaps?

'Not really,' my friend told me when I suggested it the other day. 'You were just posh!'

Unfortunately, we, in the gay community, can fixate on how we look, thinking that all we're worth is our muscle. It is a sad reality of some gay people's mentality that we think that we will only be attractive to someone if we look as close to an underwear model as possible. Of course, different if we just want sex and therefore want to show what we look like naked. It's rare, however, that this is done in a healthy way. I have done it myself – sent nude pictures from a place of desperately wanting to be validated and wanted.

I believe that body consciousness and body shame is becoming a bigger and bigger problem in the LGBTQ+ community, but we just don't talk about it. We don't talk about how we can shame ourselves, on an hourly basis, about the way we look. It can destroy our confidence and become another tool we use to bash ourselves over the head.

I felt terribly body conscious when I was in the West End show *Strictly Ballroom*. All the boy dancers had such wonderful physiques and I felt unattractive in comparison. Note the comparison game flaring up! I wanted to turn up to one of the pre-show warm-ups wearing only my pants, making a statement that I was doing it because I was so body conscious. However, when it came to it, a) I was too ashamed; b) It might not have been the most contained thing to do anyway.

Overworking – obsession with work is common, and it can act as a distraction from what is lacking in other areas of our lives. Often, when I check in with my therapist, I go through various areas of my life to see how I am doing: work, friends, relationships, spiritually and family. Work should be one of the categories, not the ONLY category.

*

I had all of the above in me, and it was a light-bulb moment when I realised it meant that I harboured a deep, spiritual wound that needed fixing. But how does one do this?

The number one tool, I have found – and I have to remind myself of it, time and time again – is to connect with others. To safely express my vulnerability. This can be in gay men's groups or it can be in 12-step groups. Group therapy, I believe, is absolutely essential to getting out the shame that has been placed onto us.

The paradox of healing shame is that the very thing we need to do is the very thing that shame stops us from doing. We need to bring ourselves into the light, while shame wants us to hide and shy away from other people and the world. Brené Brown is extremely good at explaining shame, and I would highly recommend her TED talk.

As I came into the light and worked through my gay shame, it began to dissipate. I found the motivating energy of anger, resistance, and disbelief at what I had lived through. I started to look outwards, toward my community. Looking at people who still needed support. I believe that gay shame is specific, and therefore needs to have some nurturing and holding within LGBTQ+ groups and spaces. I had to feel safe to be able to say things that, I felt, heterosexual people wouldn't understand.

During my time in Khiron House, a lot of painful work went on, and at one stage, I was working so hard in my sessions that I developed shingles, and I burst a blood vessel in my eye on more than one occasion. My nervous system was working overtime, and it really took its toll on my body. There were extra-curricular activities that we could all do outside the house, from horse therapy to craniosacral therapy. One of these that cropped up was breath work. I wasn't quite sure what it meant, but one of the residents who had done it said it was very beneficial, so off I trotted one Thursday lunchtime, to the garden shed of a very pleasant woman in north Oxford. What occurred there was that, through my breathing, I ended up, to all intents and purposes, rebirthing myself. God knows what was going on, but when the session finished I felt drained and rather relaxed. Thanking the woman for a fantastic 'birthing experience', I gently walked back to the house, deciding to go through town. This walk ended up being a very peculiar, yet incredible turn of events, that led to me working through the leftovers of my gay shame.

As I turned into the top of the high street, by a shop called Crabtree & Evelyn, I spotted Thom Yorke from Radiohead. I knew he lived in Oxford, and went over to say hello. He nodded rather curtly and I was more than happy with that response from someone as musically iconic as he. Feeling even more buoyant, after not only a rebirthing but a run-in with Thom Yorke, I sauntered on toward Boots, where I saw three guys in their mid-teens surrounding a busker. The busker was holding a harp, and I thought he was probably a nerdy student from Oxford. The guys were clearly intimidating, so I thought I would gently step in.

'Hey guys,' I said, and turned to the busker. 'Wow! That's a cool instrument; is that a harp? Were you guys wondering the same thing?'

The trio began to mutter and then decided to turn their attention fully to me.

'Hey, you're that singer, aren't you?' one of them said.

'Yeah, from *The X Factor*, innit,' said another.

'I am,' I replied. 'I'm Will Young.'

What I wanted to add was, 'I've just been rebirthed, bitches, and actually, it was *Pop Idol*, not *The X Factor*.' But I decided, for the sake of simplicity, that I wouldn't.

'Urrrrghhh! You're that batty boy, aren't you?' one of the teenagers said.

'Yeah, you're that faggot! Urrgghhh! You're disgusting. Batty boy, batty boy!'

Well, as you can imagine, this wasn't the most ideal situation post-rebirthing, and, I noted, the harp nerd wasn't helping in the slightest. So, in I launched.

'You can't actually say that anymore,' I said. 'This is offensive and illegal, and if you want to, I can walk up to the police station with you and we can talk to the police about it.'

'Yeah, whatever, poof. Urrgghhhh! Batty boy, bum boy, faggot. You're disgusting, man.'

I repeated my offer to walk with them to the police station, and they played ball for about five yards. After that, they stopped, rounding on me and getting a bit more aggressive. It was then that I decided to employ a tactic I'd wanted to try for some time. I shouted at the top of my voice to the whole high street.

'HELLO, MY NAME IS WILL YOUNG, AND THESE THREE BOYS ARE CALLING ME A FAGGOT, HOMOPHOBICALLY ATTACKING ME, AND BEING AGGRESSIVE!'

The three guys Lost. Their. Shit! They didn't know what to do. They started screaming and shouting at me.

'I'm going to fuck your mum. I'm going to rape your mum. I'm going to fuck you up.'

Me again: 'HEY, EVERYBODY! THEY ARE NOW TELLING ME THAT THEY ARE GOING TO FUCK MY MUM, AND RAPE HER, AND FUCK ME UP!'

It was the most fascinating of experiments. The whole street literally turned their attention onto these three boys, with the mood of the entire street changing. One man came up, aggressively telling the boys to 'shut up' before threatening to attack them. A woman came over and was absolutely foul-mouthed toward them. It was wonderful! What I found so fascinating was that, if this had occurred a couple of years back, the public might not have seen it as offensive and downright wrong. What I witnessed, however, was how the mood had changed. People were standing up and saying, 'This doesn't happen in this city and this country.'

My tactic had been a huge success, so every time the boys got within three yards of me, I would just start screaming, unashamedly. They followed me for a bit longer and then finally gave up.

I did then go to the police, who were brilliant, trying their hardest to find and identify the boys, but ultimately they couldn't. When I got back to the house, I didn't actually feel too bad, if a little weary. What with the rebirthing, it had been a busy afternoon.

The next day, I bought the incident up in my session with Vijay (who I called the Space Cowboy.) Vijay and I worked somatically, which, in my kindergarten description, means that I would sense into my body, and release the stored traumatic tension trapped there. Vijay thought this incident was a good thing to explore, and the resulting session was one of the most difficult of my life.

With complete consent, and with both therapist and client being utterly aware of boundaries and my cap-abilities, Vijay took on the role of the three homophobic bullies in the street the day before. Vijay sat at one end of the basement room of the house, and I sat at the other. After checking I was happy with the distance between us, he then took on the language and, effectively, the form of the homophobic kids.

He sucked his teeth. 'Hey batty boy, arse bandit, batty boy batty boy ... '

I felt the shame rise up in me. It was like a cloud to begin with, taking over my whole torso and then spreading over my face and head, forming a sort of fog. It vibrated with so much energy that it was almost suffocating

'Faggot, batty boy, poofter, arse muncher. You're disgusting man. Urrghhh! You suck dick and put dicks in your mouth. BATTY BOY!'

I felt the cloud turn to a black tarry substance in my stomach. My legs were beginning to wobble. Even now, I'm trying to remain really and truly grounded to take myself back to that time; it became almost unbearable.

Vijay apologised. He felt awful doing it, and told me so, just so he could maintain that therapist connection and support me in the overwhelming shame and self-disgust that was coming. He checked if I was OK, and I nodded; then he started to practise boundaries, advancing slowly towards me. I stood up from my chair and told him to stop, firmly holding my arms out straight, and making sure I could feel my feet on the ground. I squeezed my hands together to find strength in my arms and stamped my feet on the floor. I found more of my voice and stated firmly and increasingly loudly, 'STOP!' Vijay encouraged me and continued with the insults. I wobbled and he supported me, suggesting again that I find strength in my arms and legs. There was some resistance but I found it again. We repeated this three or four times: the cycles of strength, then doubt and weakness. It went round and round, and then, when I had firmly found a place of continued strength, I began to voice, giving back the shame that was being cast onto me.

'THIS IS NOT MY SHAME.' I spoke firmly with resonance and belief. 'THIS IS NOT MY SHAME. I HAND

IT BACK TO YOU. THIS IS NOT MY SHAME. THIS HAS BEEN PUT ONTO ME, AND I WILL NOT ACCEPT IT. I HAND IT BACK WITH LOVE AND EMPATHY AND POWER AND ABSOLUTE CONVICTION AND RESOLUTENESS.'

I wavered again and again, but found my strength and continued these words. Then there was the final piece, which is what I call 'a completion piece', something that, in somatic experiencing, brings back a different and empowering result. It is a technique used in trauma work, where we take ourselves into our body and our imagination, back to a place of helplessness and hopelessness, and then determine a different outcome. It allows the traumatic narrative and energy to 'complete', finding a different story, and a new freeing ending for ourselves and our bodies. It is a felt sense, and shows our nervous system that we *can* experience a different outcome.

It is important, at this juncture, to introduce a caveat. Often, the imagined and felt sense that happens in a differently formed outcome doesn't mean this will happen in real life. What I mean by this, and specifically to my sessions, was that often my ending would be of gladiator-ial proportions! An example. When I did work on a terrifying teacher at my prep school, I found myself imagining myself at one end of a football pitch with a group of boys standing behind me. Next to me were my dogs, past and present; especially prominent was my brother's Siberian husky/German shepherd, who looks like a white wolf. As well as her, there was an enormous Alsatian called Martha, who used to stray onto the football pitch from a local farm. I stood there resolute and firm. The teacher, who had terrorised me at Horris Hill, approached, red-faced and furious. He advanced, and I stopped him with a flick of a finger. I was so powerful, firm and protective in front of these children, while, weirdly, I seemed to be 11 years old but also an adult at the same time. I felt so strong that I could have simply swept my arm up, and he would have flown off the football pitch, out into oblivion. In the final part of the vision I sliced his head clean off with a samurai sword. God knows where the sword came from, but that doesn't matter, it was my imagination and my empowering dream. We all have dreams where we can fly or can run super fast. It's of course, not real, and I did not and WILL not cut anyone's head off!

I was astonished at where my mind had taken me; the feeling was astounding. It had taken me two years to gain that strength and to feel that power, and now I'd proved to myself that I had it in me. It had brought up a protective nature in me, as well some ferocious animal instincts. I was like a lioness! When harnessed, that strength and assuredness was more powerful than I had ever imagined, and I believe it's something we all have within us.

When it came to finding a conclusion for the deep shame that had been put on me for years and years, I ended up becoming an eagle. This is something that is often explored within shamanism. We take on forms of animals and use what they represent for us. I was always obsessed with the giant eagles in *The Hobbit*, to the point that when I watched it with my friend at an IMAX cinema in London, 3D glasses firmly on, I stood up when the eagles turned up toward the end and proclaimed, 'The eagles are here! The eagles are here!'

My friend sank down into her seat and whispered to me, 'They're not real, William.'

'Sarah,' I replied, 'who hurt you?'

When I took on the form of a giant eagle in my session with Vijay, I picked up all the shame that I had extracted from my body, held it in my talons, and flew it up towards the sun, where I released it, watching the sun burn it clear away. I soared back down over the high street and swept my giant wings, blowing the homophobic thugs away, watching them roll down the high street. After the session, I felt elated. It wasn't an ultimate cure and I still had to work on the shame, continuing to reduce it, extract it and burn it away.

My rebirthing had led me into a situation that ultimately allowed me to process a bucket load of shame. It still lives within me and there have been times where it is still activated, but the traumatic energy has been reduced, and now, it's much more contained.

Who knew a rebirthing session, Thom Yorke, a harpist and an eagle would lead to me actually becoming more empowered in myself.

CHAPTER EIGHT

Facing Our Shit

Roots are hard to dig out. The longer the tree has been there, the deeper and wider and more firmly set they are. When digging up a tree, one has to do it at the right time. For a rose it is when all the leaves are lost. The flowers are gone and the leaves have fallen. It's then that one must delicately dig around the plant to get a big 'root ball' out and to support the plant as much as possible. It is then gently wrapped in hessian and transported to be replanted into a large hole with beautifully nutritious compost, and watered plentifully, so when the sun comes out and the temperature rises in spring, the plant can, through photosynthesis, bring energy and life to its stems. Buds will form, and insects and weeds must be kept firmly and methodically at bay, but once those buds begin to open, the flowers can produce perfume-like smells, nectar and life for bees and other insects, which in turn create life through pollinating other plants. The newly planted and restored plant as it flourishes not only has inner nourishment as well as outer beauty, it will also have long-lasting and far-reaching effects it could never dream of.

Before we move into looking at our internalised shame, we have to get to a point where we have shed the outer layers that have protected us. This is when modified forms of behaviour and being no longer work. Gently peeling back the layers of pain and hurt can lead us to feeling we are losing ourselves. We don't know who we are. We don't know the world we live in. It is then that we need to find support, nourishment, understanding and guidance. We need it to navigate our way through the pain and fear of processing our inner world to make sense of the outer world, both past and present.

Connections and support networks delicately dig out our roots; they put a warm layer around us, and move us into a place of nourishment, allowing us to see and experience an environment that will allow us to shine. We learn new protective measures, and through living authentically and truthfully to ourselves, we end up exporting love and empathy into the world, which lives on, constantly regenerating and re-energising.

Today I am off to my local charity shop, which raises money for people with HIV and AIDS. I started bringing clothes into the shop when I moved to the area. As I slowly drip fed the place with every item of clothing I possessed that didn't fit me anymore (I was on a Marie Kondo blitz), I began to realise I felt really safe there. It's solely occupied by LBGTQ+ people, but also people who have mental health obstacles. As soon as I walk in the door, it's like stepping into a haven for me.

Traditionally, of course, the clubbing life was an area where one could feel safe. And safety was and is essential. It's essential to be in a space logistically where one might meet other gay people to form relationships with, be they sexual, loving, or a friendship. However, nightlife can become very murky. It can allow us to lose inhibitions, but also to fall down a slippery path of escape and denial, running away from our pain and hurt, and indulging in toxic behaviour. It can also be a lot of fun, and for those who are not using alcohol, drugs and sex simply as a plaster to cover old wounds, it is a wonderfully uplifting and resourcing thing. I have to admit, my relationship with alcohol and drugs has, at times, been one of avoidance rather than one of simple pleasure.

As I've got older, I've realised the importance of connecting with other LGBTQ+ people on a level that doesn't involve clubbing, sex or mind-altering substances. In my younger years, the idea of being in a gay choir or playing for the gay water polo team filled me with dread, and actually stirred up a lot internalised homophobia in me. I couldn't think why people would do that kind of thing; it all felt rather student-like. I realise now, however, that it is essential to be around other LGBTQ+ people, in a space that hasn't been enforced by a heteronormative society.

Going into other realms of safety and connection is a really positive thing for me, so today I'm dressing the windows of this local charity shop. I admit, I feel some shame writing this. I have become the type of person who needs to be around other broken people. How has my life got to this? What a loser! Actually, it's more about connection than anything. I don't trust people because I wasn't brought up to trust people. Consequently, I sometimes feel lonely, uncertain and unwanted. These feelings are natural and often come up as we move towards healing. I even feel shame writing this down, which is why it's important.

It's important because the shame is always lurking there and can rear its head in what seems the most innocuous of situations. We have to, time and time again, bet it out of our bodies, out of our nervous system and out of our psyches. Old wounds create neural pathways that fire off well-trodden routes in our bodies. These well-travelled roads are deep grooves that have repeatedly run to dead ends of shame. The good news is we can create new roads that lead to healthier and wondrous destinations. We can put in gentle yet firm roadblocks on the historical routes and create new exit points. I promise you this is biological fact!

A way of creating ownership and an understanding of our tougher feelings is to build our self-esteem and self-belief by owning our truth and remaining authentic to ourselves. By not being true to ourselves and showing our inner world, we are actually shutting the people we love out. It takes time to realise that what we feel and think is valuable and completely valid. How we act on this is a different thing. This can be anything from daily issues with people we know to moving into a public space. We must always feel safe to be able to express ourselves and something I have learnt is to check myself.

Being a public figure, I don't have to shove every little detail in people's faces, but, on the other hand, I shouldn't have to modify my behaviour just because it makes others uncomfortable. For me, it is a moveable feast. It's about a balance and maintaining a sense of empathy and forgiveness, along with a desire to perhaps educate.

While I was interviewing Skin, the frontwoman of the band Skunk Anansie, she said the most wonderful thing. Talking about being a black woman living in the countryside, she commented that many of the locals would never have even experienced living with a black woman in their community before. She made the point that people sometimes get things wrong: using the wrong language, or maybe displaying a lack of understanding or open-mindedness. She said we should 'give people a minute ... '

In other words, rather than rushing in, feeling outraged and disgusted and going on the attack, just give them a minute to catch up. This phrase has really stuck with me.

The reality is that on a wider more public level there is a shit ton of homophobia and prejudice that lives under the surface. I could get outraged every minute of every day. There have been times when I have felt extremely militant in my anger towards heterosexual people, but this isn't useful, and it's normally driven by fear.

The second time I interviewed Skin was on the radio, and we spoke about Pride and the idea of it becoming corporate, with big companies using Pride as a marketing tool. Skin was very pragmatic and measured in her response. She said that many countries she's travelled to long for such exposure and financial support from businesses. She believes we are in a privileged position in the West that we can even debate these issues, yet it is making the LGBTQ+ community turn on itself, and causing segregation within the community: transgender, bisexual, black and ethnic groups etc. We are privileged to be in our position, but we sometimes talk ourselves into loops and dead ends, which end up creating conflict and a lack of love and support. We need to recognise the privilege; recognise how wonderful it is that we have freedom of expression, and then consolidate as queer people.

I actually have a problem with the word acceptance. Now, aged 41, I don't want to be 'accepted' by others. I don't want to be accepted by people who merely attempt a begrudging U-turn. In fact, I couldn't give a shit what people's inhibited thinking is. The actor Andrew Scott has spoken of not wanting to be known as 'freely or openly living as a gay man' and I completely agree with him. It denotes that there is some sort of other option – to NOT live openly and freely, hiding and being fearful of rejection and acceptance in the winder world.

If there is a lack of acceptance, we have to look at why some non-LGBTQ+ people feel threatened. Is it because they feel insecure about their own sexuality and gender? Is there something about a gay man that forces certain people to question themselves? Damn right there is! By not being within the heteronormative world, and indeed not adhering to those rules, I believe we spark something in some heterosexual people. We make them feel uncomfortable, forcing them to look at their own desires, and to experience people who aren't conforming: who have to beat their own drum, and who are brave enough to own that part of who they are, despite it leading to a life of exposure and vulnerability. Suddenly, especially for some straight men, their masculinity is tested. The shoe is on the other foot. They're confronted by a man who sleeps with men. Their power has gone. The power of lusting after and ruling over woman with masculine prowess and athletic dominance is threatened by a man who lusts after men. They are put in a position where they imagine they might be ogled or be objectified. The patriarchal order is being challenged and they are terrified. Gay women are even more of a threat to some straight men; they challenge their masculinity by not being interested in them sexually. I believe gay women suffer from latent prejudice because of this.

The reaction to these challenges has, in the past, been to put LGBTQ+ people in their place. Exclude them from legal rights and human rights. Belittle them and make damn sure they cannot rise up to dethrone the chauvinistic rule.

Luckily, there are plenty of heterosexual men who are secure and accepting of themselves, their vulnerabilities, their humanity, and therefore of others. Those men have no problem with difference. In fact, they often welcome it.

The introduction of civil partnerships, and ultimately, gay marriage, were wonderful things, and great leaps forward. I can't remember if I was in a relationship at the time gay marriage became legal, but I do remember thinking how amazing it was that I was now free to marry a person I was in love with, just like my straight friends and family. My theory about gay relationships, prior to that, was that you'd be with someone for a while, then you'd move in together, get a dog, and after that you'd start sleeping around. To me, gay marriage made it possible for same-sex relationships to progress past getting a dog. There was an end point, whatever that might be; something to aim for. With gay marriage came empowerment and visibility. There was also protection under the law and the recognition that gay couples could be a legally recognised family. Now, if something happened to one's partner, their family weren't able to swoop in and make all the decisions, which had been the case before. Of course, some queer people still believe that marriage is a heteronormative thing that they shouldn't have to take on, and I understand that argument too.

The problem with shame is that it leads us into the very place that stops us wanting to connect. As gay men we are prevented from being our authentic selves by a deluge of disgust and fear that is thrown onto us, which, in turn, becomes internalised. We turn in on ourselves, believing that it must be us that's at fault, the evidence thrust upon us leads us to no other conclusion and a 'shame vortex' is created.

Our lack of safety and ability to freely express and be supported and nurtured allows shame to set into our very soul. To expunge all these painful feelings and belief systems we need to see that now we *are* able to be safe. How we *are not* the ones at fault and, in the present day, we *are* able to validate ourselves and disseminate the system of the heteronormative world that has led us to such toxic and debilitating states.

When we try to connect authentically, we will always come up against the things that have stopped us connecting in that way in the first place. It is the pain and the suffering that held us back; the feeling that we don't belong. In finding our strength and our own personal power we will have setbacks. It forces us to face our shit.

I have so much desire for the future. I think that we are letting down our young people by not educating and supporting them in schools. Too often we rest as adults on how far we have come, yet we forget the atmosphere of shame and quiet toxic prejudice that still percolates in the education system and is completely negated by government. I also feel that transgender people are now being attacked and experience prejudice as people see that as a new acceptable form of homophobia, and this is one of the key things to focus on. Right now, there are not enough much-needed support groups out there, but interest and awareness around gay shame is growing. Still, more could be done. We must connect with our brothers and sisters, and, together, with support and guidance, be led through the sea of shame so that we might embrace our vulnerabilities and, through this, find true empowerment to recapture our souls.

I would like to see groups set up for LGBTQ+ people to work through their shame and to heal wounds that they neither asked for nor deserved. There is a huge lack of these types of restorative collectives, and I have a desire to help create some.

I had no objectives in this book other than to connect with my own story through rediscovering what my experiences have been throughout my life knowing I was a gay person. Through my connection with myself I had some hopes that others might feel they aren't alone. Hopes are different to objectives, or perhaps better explained expectations. A friend told me once that to share one story in a pure and authentic way with no expectations of how the audience or reader will react is THE BEST WAY to connect. It would be manipulative of me to try to affect what you the reader will feel and get out of this book; it is however my hope that you will get something. Comfort, joy, clarity . . . it is for you to have that experience. Whatever it is I thank you for taking the time to read my story on what it has been like to be a gay man.

Epilogue

I't's my friend's fortieth. We're eating upstairs in a restaurant's private dining room. I'm especially pleased with what I have chosen to wear: some wide crinkled black shorts that almost look like a skirt, in black, of course, and a sleeveless layered black floaty top. Also in black. I'm also wearing black DM boots. I don't think I'm in mourning although I have decided this attire would be wonderful for any funeral. I'm pleased for many reasons. I feel very masculine and sexy, yet also feminine and sexy. I'd mused in the mirror an hour previously, that I was now at a stage where I felt like I was really expressing who I am as a person. I don't really care what people think of me; I just want to be authentic to myself. In amongst all this, I still felt terribly anxious about the evening ahead. Social anxiety is something I've always felt. I'm not sure if I can relate it to growing up gay, but it is there and I just have to handle it as best I can.

At the table, I take the opportunity to look around at the assembled company. I'm sitting with two gay women either side of me. Their journeys to being where they currently are with their sexuality have been very different. Opposite is the birthday boy and his husband. He was the first ever man to mention his husband in an Oscar speech. To his right are his friends, who are a heterosexual couple, and to his left is an American man with a moustache and a kilt. I am, of course, immediately supportive and delighted at the kilt.

I look around, and despite my earlier anxious state, I think about how great it is that I'm now in a place I never thought I would get to; hanging out with such a brilliant mix of people ... to be with other gay men and women, and for it to be so natural, with us all simply existing together, and enjoying each other's company.

Appendix

APPENDIX 1:

CBT Techniques

Connection is one of the keys to building our self-confidence. We must find our tribe. It is terrifying to begin with.

There is a great CBT technique I learnt that helps with this:

1. Before going to something write down out of 10 how scared you are
2. Write down out of 10 how well you will think it will go
3. Write down out of 10 how you think you will feel afterwards

After the event:

1. Write down out of 10 how you did feel during the event
2. Write down how you now feel after the event

Then look at your projected numbers on how you thought it would go and how you thought you would feel afterwards and compare them.

There is no right or wrong; it is a useful exercise that helps you in times of panic and can slowly allow your brain to see that the way you think you might feel won't actually end up being the case

Another technique I use that you might find useful is the ten-minute rule: I tell myself I will give myself ten minutes at a place and if things haven't calmed by then then I can leave. Alongside this, a great thing to remember is that you don't HAVE to go to anything. Once I realise that, often I calm down and feel more relaxed about going.

APPENDIX 2:

Help and Support

There are so many great charities and support networks in the UK you can turn to if you are struggling with any of the issues I have spoken about in this book. I have listed a small selection below, but there are many more available online if you can't find what you're looking for here:

LGBT Foundation
Provides a wide range of services to support lesbian, gay, bisexual and trans people.
https://lgbt.foundation/
03453 303030

London Friend

For those in and around London, supporting the mental wellbeing of LGBT people.

https://londonfriend.org.uk/

020 7833 1674

Mermaids

Charity supporting young trans people as well as their families.

https://www.mermaidsuk.org.uk/

0808 801 0400

MindLine Trans+

Helpline for LGBT+ people who identify as transgender, agender, gender fluid, and non-binary. Also supports families.

https://bristolmind.org.uk/help-and-counselling/mindline-transplus/

0300 123 3393

Mind Out

LGBTQ+ mental health service.

https://www.mindout.org.uk/

01273 234839

Peter Tatchell Foundation

Foundation protecting and promoting human rights.

https://www.petertatchellfoundation.org/

Sex and Love Addicts Anonymous

LGBT-friendly and also LGBT-specific meetings.

https://www.slaauk.org/

Stonewall

Campaigning and lobbying group.

https://www.stonewall.org.uk/

0800 0502020

Switchboard LGBT Helpline

Mental health helpline for LBGT+ people.

https://switchboard.lgbt/help/

0300 330 0630

Terrence Higgins Trust

HIV and sexual health charity.

https://www.tht.org.uk/

0808 802 1221

Further Reading

Below is a list of some of the books and pieces of writing that have helped and inspired me on this journey:

Bradshaw, John, *Healing the Shame that Binds You*, Health Communications, 2006

Cleto, Professor Fabio, 'The Spectacles of Camp', *Camp: Notes on Fashion*, Yale University Press, 2019

Odets, Walt, *Out of the Shadows: Reconstructing Gay Men's Lives*, Penguin, 2019

Sontag, Susan, 'Notes on Camp', *Against Interpretation and Other Essays*, Farrar Straus & Giroux, 1966

Tatchell, Peter, *AIDS: A Guide to Survival*, Gay Men's Press, 1990

Todd, Matthew, *Straight Jacket: How to be Gay and Happy*, Transworld, 2016

Acknowledgements

To all at Ebury, thank you for your belief that writing this book was a possibility and thank you for your continued support and enthusiasm and dedication to what this book represents.

Thank you to Adrian for helping me find my passion in wellbeing and encouraging me to put this down on paper.

Index

WY indicates Will Young.